DISCARDED

Furniture
by Architects

Furniture
by Architects

Foreword by Stephen Crafti

images
Publishing

Published in Australia in 2013 by
The Images Publishing Group Pty Ltd
ABN 89 059 734 431
6 Bastow Place, Mulgrave, Victoria 3170, Australia
Tel: +61 3 9561 5544 Fax: +61 3 9561 4860
books@imagespublishing.com
www.imagespublishing.com

Copyright © The Images Publishing Group Pty Ltd 2013
The Images Publishing Group Reference Number: 1069

National Library of Australia Cataloguing-in-Publication entry:
Title: Furniture by architects / edited by Driss Fatih.
ISBN: 9781864705041 (hbk.)
Subjects: Furniture design.
                 Architect-designed furniture.
Dewey number   749.2

Edited by Driss Fatih

Designed by The Graphic Image Studio Pty Ltd, Mulgrave, Australia
www.tgis.com.au

Pre-publishing services by United Graphic Pte Ltd, Singapore

Printed by Everbest Printing Co. Ltd., in Hong Kong/China on 150gsm Quattro Silk Matt

IMAGES has included on its website a page for special notices in relation to this
and our other publications. Please visit www.imagespublishing.com.

Front cover photography: Foscarini
Back cover photography: Ditte Isager, styling by Christine Rudolph

Contents

Foreword

Architects are increasingly designing furniture as clients seek bespoke interiors, customised to their needs. Architects such as Le Corbusier made an enormous contribution to this field in the 1920s, with his distinctive lounges and armchairs. Framed in chrome, they continue to form part of the contemporary interior. Architect Josef Hoffman also made his mark a few decades before, with his Modernist furniture to suit modernist times. Whether a lounge, armchair, credenza, light fitting or desk, architects often prefer to design something to fit an interior rather than visit a furniture showroom. Sometimes, an architect's design may be the result of a gap in the market.

This book beautifully illustrates bespoke design by architects. Some of the materials used are ancient, while others are high-tech. Saaj Design's table is made from a 10,000-year-old fallen red gum log. Architect Brian Steendyk's Anise Pendant, evocative of Middle Eastern lanterns, also speaks of the past, while creating a contemporary form.

Some of the world's leading architects, including Foster + Partners and architect Zaha Hadid are included in this book. The 520 Armchair by Foster + Partners for Walter Knoll is constructed in three flat patterns. Appearing as a hand-drawn sketch, this armchair has the texture and comfort found in a traditional leather armchair. Zaha Hadid Design's Liquid Glacial Dining and Coffee Table, made from polished clear Plexiglas, capture the spirit of her architecture, with their distinctive fluid lines. These pieces reveal the waves and ripples below the surface, like water frozen in time.

As ethereal are the Light Boxes designed by Griffin Enright Architects. Made from eco-resin, with embedded seagrass, these lights create a soft glow. The idea of the beach is also evoked by architect Marcus O'Reilly's Flotsam + Jetsam series, a range of tables made from driftwood. Combined with black steel frames, there's a tension between the slick and the rustic.

One of the many highlights in the book is a credenza, designed by Johnson Chou. Glowing from within, the curiosity-style cabinet includes 17 acrylic cube-like partitions that unfold when the door is opened. From the permanent to the occasional, there is even a Christmas tree in the book. Rather than chopping down a tree every year, the architect Vladimir Ivanov came up with the idea of a flat-packed tree, made from birch plywood. Complete with circular cut-outs, there's even space to dangle decorations.

This book features so many items for the home and outdoors. And while some architects simply design one-off pieces, most of these designs can be enjoyed by people other than clients, who are looking for something unique. There's something in this book for all lovers of great design.

Stephen Crafti
Architecture & Design Writer and Critic

Architect

Inspired

Furniture

Allegro Lamp
atelier oï

Design team	atelier oï
Dimensions	Maximum height 500cm Allegro vivace diameter 64cm Allegro ritmico diameter 75cm Allegro assai diameter 136cm
Material	Extruded aluminium, Halogen energy saver 1 x 230W, Halogen 1 x 100W
Colours	Allegro vivace: brown Allegro ritmico: black Allegro assai: gold

A group of lines create an elegant, fascinating symphony in a suspended, almost magical equilibrium and give life to a new lamp designed to feature in large public and private spaces. Aluminium elements flow and combine together to give the suspension a light, bodiless effect. As well as illuminating rooms with a pleasant effect of light and shade, the lamp has a hidden and slightly mobile nature. Oscillation makes the aluminium elements vibrate and emit a soft, magical sound. This musicality has inspired its names – Allegro vivace, Allegro ritmico and Allegro assai – three versions in different sizes and colours that can also be personalised on request.

When used alone or in a group, Allegro is ideal for creating a visual focal point in any environment. It characterises and enhances architecture, thanks to the complexity of its language and its interpretation of materials, shapes and volumes. It gives a diffused downward light that reflects off the ceiling.

Photography by Foscarini

Anise Pendant
design brian steendyk

Throwing a constellation through its etched
pattern onto the walls, the Anise Pendant
is both simple and beautiful. To shroud the
light source, the anise diamond apertures
crescendo from small at the centre to large
at the extremities. The lightshade is fabricated
from a single delicate sheet of etched brass,
ensuring minimal waste and providing an
elegant addition to any space.

Photography by Brian Steendyk

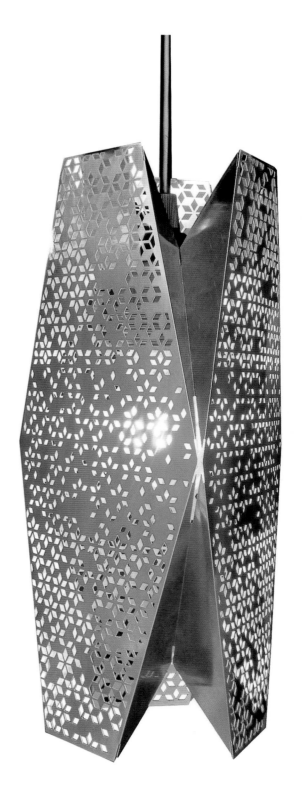

Dimensions   H28/60 x W145/254cm
(small/large)

Materials   Brass, blackened brass

AR-K Cupboard
Objects by Estudio Carme Pinós

The AR-K is a cupboard made from assembled wooden pieces, suspended on the wall. Liberating the ground of obstacles, it creates a sensation of amplitude in the space in which it sits. The steel shelves are adjustable and can be used as a shelf or a coat hanger, adapting themselves to different storage necessities. The panels are cut by laser.

AR-K is available in two sizes: AR-K LARGE and AR-K SMALL. It is possible to add extra shelves for the LARGE model – up to a maximum of eight.

Design	Carme Pinós
Dimensions	W71.5 x D38.5 x L58cm (AR-K SMALL)
	W71.5 x D57 x L160cm (AR-K LARGE)
Weight	18.85–20.4kg (whole set, including two shelves) (AR-K SMALL)
	48.4–53.95kg (whole set, including four shelves) (AR-K LARGE)
Material	Laminated birch wood or coloured high-density fibreboard (HDF)
Colour	Black and blue or black and orange, varnished; varnished laminated birch timber

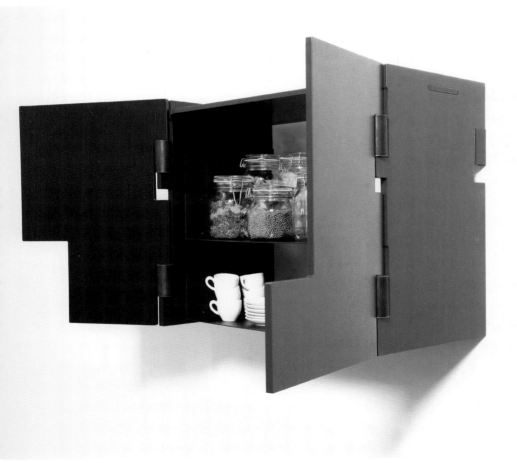

Arc Table

Foster + Partners for Molteni & C

The Arc table is the latest addition to a range of products designed by Foster + Partners for Molteni & C, Milan. Drawing inspiration from tensile fabric structures, its form is generated by software developed to create flowing architectural designs. The sculptural base is a single sweeping form anchored by three legs – between each extension, the material curves upwards to balance the tabletop. The top is a tempered glass disc, measuring either 140 or 150 centimetres in diameter, and is available in an extra light finish. Three thin stainless steel plates are UV-bonded to the glass and allow the base to be safely and discreetly secured using just three small screws.

Early prototypes used self-skinning polyurethane foam and aluminium to determine the form the base of the table would take. However, for production, the design team investigated the possible use of 'Ductal', a self-coloured, lightweight fibre-filled concrete material previously used by the practice for building projects. Its strength and comparative lightness presented an interesting paradox and the material can be moulded to allow the wall thickness and details to be accurately controlled. Ductal is also waterproof and the mass-coloured base ensures the colour stays fresh throughout its lifespan.

There are several stages in the technical development and production process: firstly, a 1:1 wooden prototype is created on a CNC machine. This model is finished in exactly the same way as a final production piece, as it forms the basis of the two shells that make up the mould. Each shell is fabricated in rubber and slotted into a steel frame. Once the two shells are locked together, the reinforced concrete is poured in through the leg section. After 24 hours, the shells are removed and the table is left to dry for 20 days, until Ductal has reached its maximum strength and the base can be finished and sealed.

Photography by Molteni

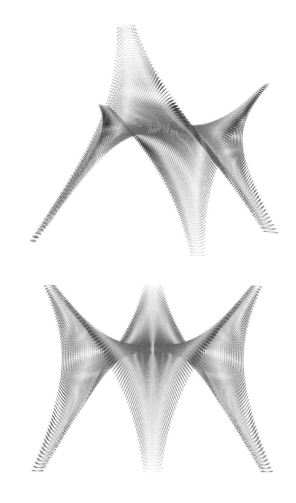

Dimensions   140/150cm diameter, H75cm

Materials   Tempered glass, stainless steel plate

Ash Ribbon Table
workshop/apd

Design team	Andrew Kotchen, Matthew Berman, Brook Quach
Dimensions	H76 x L323 x W112cm
Materials	Solid ash, cold rolled steel

The Ash Ribbon table marries the organic and industrial in a contemporary dining table with its naturally curved solid ash edges and a sculptural steel base and ribbon centre. Used as either a dining table or a conference table, this piece of furniture is both rustic and modern. At 112cm wide and more than 3 metres long, this table seats 12 comfortably. Each piece is unique and available in several sizes and finishes.

Photography by Donna Dotan Photography

Athlone Bench

keith williams architects

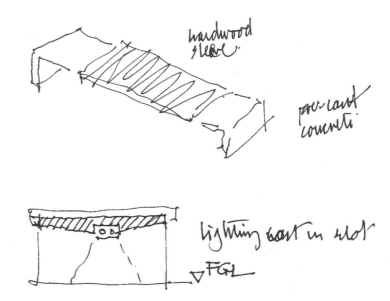

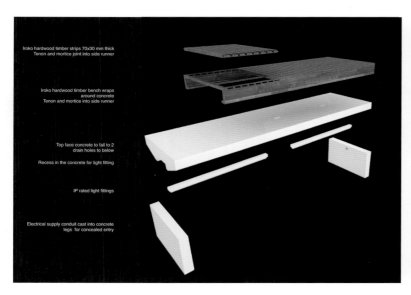

Iroko hardwood timber strips 70x30 mm thick
Tenon and mortice joint into side runner

Iroko hardwood timber bench wraps
around concrete
Tenon and mortice into side runner

Top face concrete to fall to 2
drain holes to below

Recess in the concrete for light fitting

IP rated light fittings

Electrical supply conduit cast into concrete
legs for concealed entry

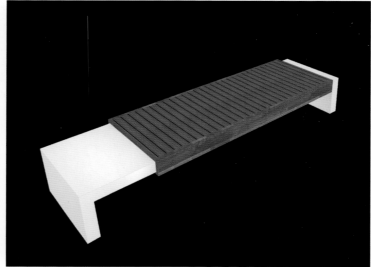

Keith Williams originally created the Athlone bench for the firm's Civic Centre project in Athlone, Ireland. The benches were laid out in the public square facing the new Civic Centre, as part of the architect's comprehensive transformation of the civic quarter of the town. The concept for the form of the seating grew from the linearity of the architectural ordering and the materiality of the Civic Centre building itself. The benches were conceived as heavy monolithic forms, reflecting the cast concrete of the Civic Centre's façades. The bench, more like a coffee table than conventional seating, is long and low and set out on a basic elevational ratio of 6:1 to achieve its elegant proportion. The finalised design takes the form of a smooth low concrete table, factory pre-cast as a single unit, on which an enveloping Iroko hardwood timber capping is placed asymmetrically, providing the seating surface and contact point with the human body.

Downlighting is set discretely in the centre of the underside of the bench to accent and underscore the benches' nighttime presence, while providing secondary lighting to the public realm. The first generation of the bench was made in grey pre-cast fine concrete for the Athlone Civic Centre project. Subsequently, for later projects by the firm, such as Clones Library and County Headquarters, Ireland and the Marlowe Theatre in Canterbury, UK, white pre-cast concrete was substituted for the original grey of natural concrete, to further refine the aesthetic of the piece.

Photography by Eamonn O'Mahony

Dimensions	H45 x L300 x W86cm
Materials	Concrete, Iroko hardwood timber

Balance Lounge Chair
Pure Design Finland

Designer	Esa Vesmanen
Dimensions	H120 x L165 x W57cm
Materials	Plywood, tubular steel, felt, TB speakers W3-871SC Amplifier ANP 32, 2x 25W
Colours	White laminate, black felt

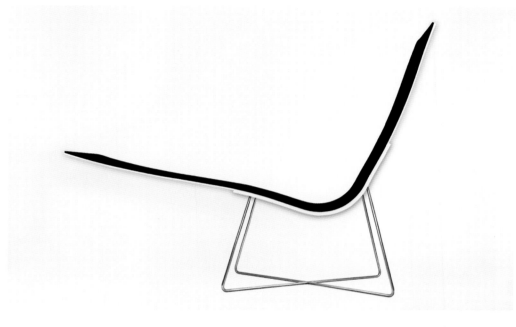

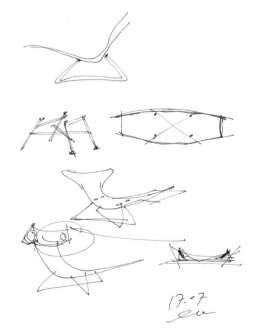

The slim lines and sensory experience of the Balance Lounge Chair inspire feelings of lightness and balance with one's surroundings. Sensuous natural materials – plywood and pure felt – are merged with quality acoustic technology to create an intimate sensory experience, in which music plays an essential role in relaxation.

Designed and manufactured in Finland, the lounge chair's lithe plywood shell follows the contours of the body and its tubular steel base imparts a light weight and decisively contemporary design. Sound can be transmitted from any Bluetooth device to an amplifier and two high-fidelity loudspeakers in the chaise longue detachable sound pillow. This system offers an unencumbered audio experience while preventing others from hearing what you are listening to. Even if you are immersed in the 'sound world' of the chair, you can hear the sounds within your environment, thus creating a more realistic experience. The sound pillow can be powered by an AC adaptor or by battery and is attached with magnets so it can be easily removed or adjusted.

"I am inspired by the basic elements of life, light and matter", says designer Esa Vesmanen. "As an interior architect and sailing enthusiast, I wanted to merge traditional furniture traditions with contemporary technology and to arouse the fundamental human response to the rippling of wind and waves. The strongest aesthetic experience – when you feel shivers down your spine – is experienced when the materials, details and atmosphere touch you".

Photography by Pekka Kiirala and Pauliina Pennanen

Bamboo Float

Swatt | Miers Architects

Swatt | Miers Architects often designs custom furniture pieces for their clients. In 1995, Robert Swatt designed a pair of sofas for his own house, constructed from glue-laminated Douglas fir beams, horizontal versions of the house's structure. The floating platform concept was roughly based on classic mid-century pieces Swatt had seen that included bench-mounted, movable wood-framed seats. In 2008 he designed a lighter-weight version, utilising bamboo plywood for the platform and legs and fully upholstered seats with self-supporting seat backs. This new line of sustainable, modular furnishings is now marketed, manufactured and sold through a licensing agreement with Viesso, Inc., in Los Angeles, California.

Photography by Russell Abraham

The books on the coffee table read:
100 more of the world's best houses
the new 100 houses

Designer   Robert Swatt
Dimensions   H38/74 (seat/back) x W76/279 (single seat/sofa) x D81cm
Materials   Bamboo, plywood

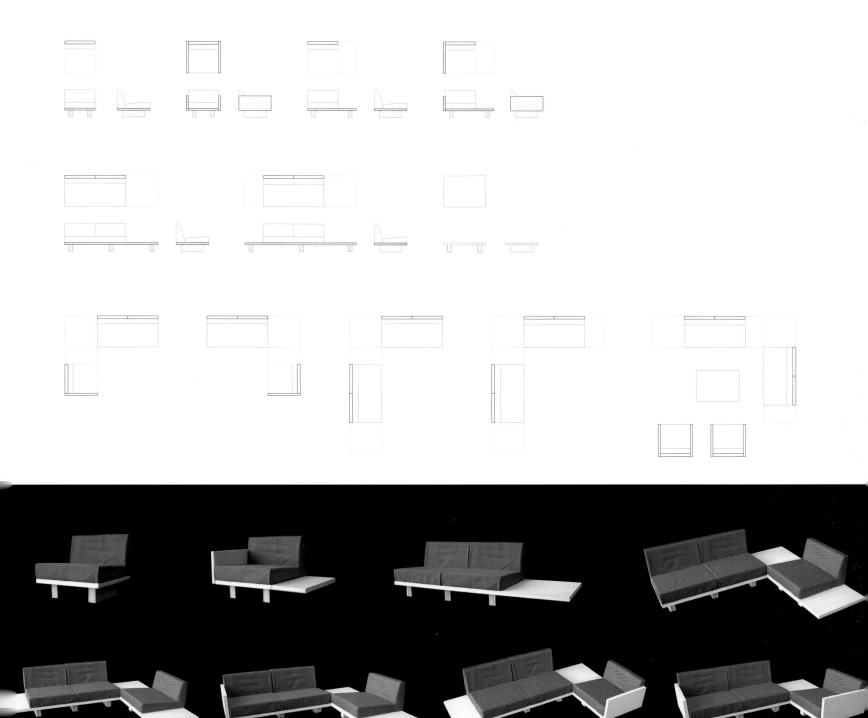

Barcode Light

AKDA – Amit Khanna Design Associates

The Barcode Light is designed as an abstraction of the 'barcode' used extensively in the commercial world today and as an integral part of all products that we use. Fabricated as a solid piece, with voids crafted to permit light through, the light is manufactured in various colours and is a notional representation of the playful nature of the solid/void relationship.

Photography by Amit Khanna

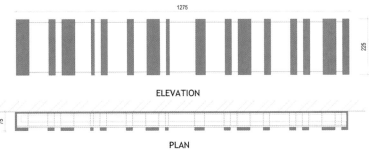

ELEVATION

PLAN

Dimensions   H23 x W128 x D8cm
Materials   Laminated plywood, frosted glass
Colours   Red, black, yellow

Black & White Sideboard, Buffet and Desk

Saaj Design

This piece is about combining a dining room buffet, a study niche and an entertainment unit. It connects the dining room with the living room. The monochromatic colour of the Calcutta marble draws the eye to the intricacies of the marble's grain. This was used to reinforce the three-dimensionality of the piece. After being selected by hand, each sheet was individually photographed and assessed. Like an origami process, two-dimensional images were used to make the three-dimensional object. The piece was technically challenging to make due to the weight of the stone used on the drawer and door faces of the storage components and the need for concealed hinges. It negates three different bench heights but reads as one continuous unit. All components appear to float off the floor level. The construction technique consisted of book matching and mitred and concealed hinges.

Photography by Andrew Bartholomeusz

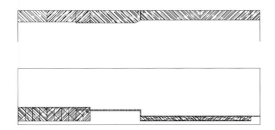

Design team	Andrew Bartholomeusz, Sally Anderson
Dimensions	H45–90 x L1210 x W50–65cm
Material	Calcutta marble

Booktrough
Holt Clifford Designers

New forms are rare, especially in the area of book storage. The booktrough, however, is a new form developed from an old idea. Early in the history of the development of the book, when they were precious and few, their storage and proximity were vastly different from the contemporary expectation of a vast gilded library of art books. This gap between image and the reality of most people was addressed in the booktrough.

In essence it is a low, useful object that can house people and new information technologies alongside books. It is made from a single sheet of custom-laid plywood. The components are the front, back, base and hidden ladder frame panels, which minimise waste and utilise the double-faced nature of the plywood and the bookbinding edge of the layered ply to infer its task.

The assembly is held together by eight fixings in its undercarriage through the electro-polished stainless steel base that supports the timber above the floor and binds the timber leaves together.

A suite of accessories is available to the user so the unit can fit or change with their needs. Ranging from simple dividers and suede bench seats to more elaborate chests and audiovisual cabinets, each piece fits into the cavity and can be assembled according to need or new location in the home. This is an object of humble construction that excels in its flexibility and appeal because of its unusual proportions and an unspoken invitation to interact with it.

Photography by Pia Photo

Dimensions H55 xW239/120 (large/small) x D42cm

Materials Custom-laid plywood, American white oak
or American walnut veneer, electro-polished
stainless steel legs, automotive suedes

Boomerang chill

Quim Larrea & Associates

Design team	Quim Larrea, Katherine Bedwell
Dimensions	Armchair: H103 x W61 x D90cm
	Chaise Longue: H103 x W61 x D150cm
Material	Solid ash wood grain, upholstery fabric

The Boomerang collection is a Scandinavian aesthetic answer to a proposal inspired by an aboriginal implement – the boomerang – taken as the backbone of the whole design.

Boomerang chill is the latest innovative piece in the Boomerang collection. Quim Larrea and his associate Katherine Bedwell completed, with great success and satisfaction, the seat family which they had already designed in 2006 for Proyec: the brand under which manufacturer Sancal sells seats, designed with meticulous care – tailored to the useability requirements of the elderly. As evidence of the attractiveness of its design, it is noteworthy that the armchair with headrest was a finalist for the Delta awards and selected for the German Designpreis.

Clean and formal simplicity, polished solid ash wood grain and carefully machined curves all showcase the noble and naturalistic crafting of a design classic. Its simple, functional and ergonomic forms make low-cost solutions available for furniture that is equally suitable for the home.

The seat, almost at ground level, leads to the use of the adjective in Boomerang chill. It is marketed under the brand Sancal as a seat for relaxing atmospheres, in which to 'chill out'. In its new format and market focus, it offers three very distinctive versions: easy chair, ottoman and chaise longue.

Photography by Marcelo Martinez (page 40) and David Frutos (page 41)

Bridge Island Bench
Saaj Design

Given the limited space available, the architect decided to explore this piece
as a functional island bench but make it appear like a piece of furniture.
The simplicity of the rolled extruded profile enables this. The openness under
the island bench resembles other elements of the living and kitchen space:
light and delicate. It also investigates scale – a macro link or ribbon loop of
the adjoining dividing screen or of the crystal pendant, so that the bench
enters the dialogue of the space. HI-MACS was selected as the material to
achieve this piece for the properties of being able to be formed and shaped
by heat welding into what appears to be a seamless extrusion. All the
structural elements are hidden from the viewer's eye.

Photography by Freeway

Design team   Andrew Bartholomeusz,
               Sally Anderson, Claire Davy
Dimensions   L340 x W100 x H90cm

Cabinet of Curiosity

Johnson Chou

Dimensions   H74 x W183 x D91cm

Materials   Acid-etched glass, acrylic,
MDF, plastic laminate

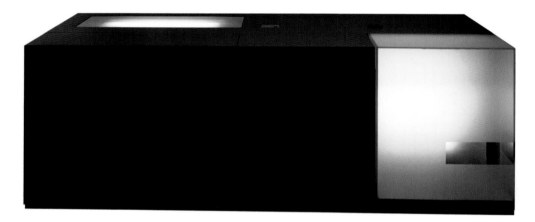

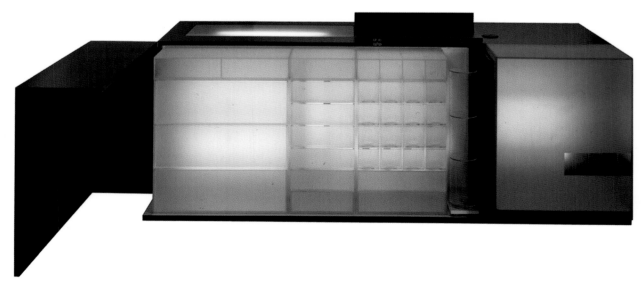

Encouraging the designer to consider the sensibilities of past centuries, the client's mandate was one of both function and whimsy – incorporating the prosaic demands of a workstation with the historical precedent of the curiosity cabinet.

Closed, the cabinet appears as a minimalist rectangular cuboid – a solid and restrained form that belies its interactive quality. On closer inspection, however, this seemingly austere, utilitarian object appears to glow from within. As it opens and the front panel swings outward, the cabinet slowly discloses its contents, revealing its inner magic. Seventeen acrylic cubes, their fronts obscured and semi-opaque, rotate 360 degrees; vitrines open, drawers slide; a three-level glass cylinder extends; the front frosted glass display case pulls outwards; and finally, from a hidden recess on top, a single cube waits to be discovered.

Once opened, the cabinet's luminous forms create an ethereal presence of perfect architectural proportions, like a glowing modernist cityscape from the future.

Encouraging active participation by simultaneously revealing and concealing, the cabinet plays on discovery and the unexpected, tantalising the imagination by making viewing a ritual and conscious act. One questions the nature and truth of not only the objects collected, but the very purpose and function of the cabinet itself. By engaging the viewer this way, Chou's cabinet remains true to the original delight of collecting.

Photography courtesy of the designer

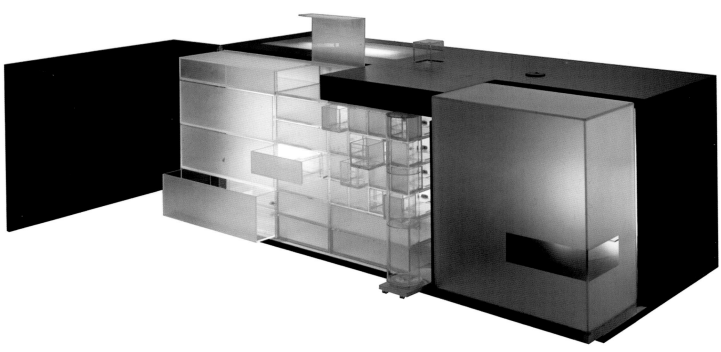

Cascade Sideboard

Saaj Design

Careful grain selection of the she-oak timber veneer enabled the sheets of veneer to become a three-dimensional lineal cascade from a dining room buffet/sideboard into a magazine store into entertainment sideboard – a link of defined spaces within an open plan. The thinness of the porcelain slab and metalwork contrast with the solidified she-oak cabinets below. They bridge from one storage block, across existing windows, anchored by bookends at both ends of the room. The bridging components are light and delicate to reinforce the floating cascade. The construction technique involved thick veneering with blind mitred dovetails and tung oil finish.

Photography by Andrew Bartholomeusz

Design team	Andrew Bartholomeusz, Sally Anderson, Claire Davy with Damien Wright Studio
Dimensions	H45–90 x L1160 x W50cm
Materials	She-oak, porcelain slab, laser-cut steel

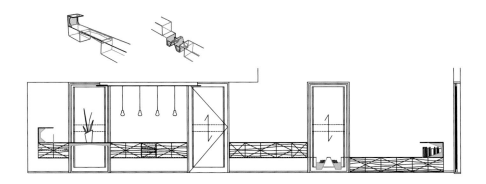

Chair Guido

Söhne & Partners Architekten

Design team	Guido Trampitsch, Thomas Baertl, Harald Guggenbichler
Dimensions	H60 x W65 x D72cm
Materials	Wooden structure, foam cushion, artificial leather and fabric upholstery

Chair Guido is a new type of chair. It combines two different kinds of chairs: the usual, elegant and mostly light restaurant chair and the heavy, cosy and comfortable lounge-chair. On the one hand, the chair invites the sitter to settle back, relax and enjoy the evening as if they are sitting on a comfortable couch. On the other hand, it encourages the sitter to eat while offering perfect seating comfort such as perfect height, firmness and inclination.

Another sign of the unique combination is that it fits exactly under the dinner table, even though it has armrests on both sides. To especially underline the lounge character of the dinner-chair,

there are no chair legs. The framework that holds the chair together is made out of wood; the surface is cushioned and overdrawn with solid fabric and artificial leather.

Chair Guido was originally designed especially for the Dinnerclub Albertina Passage in Vienna, and evolved in co-operation with the architects' partners at Guggenbichler Design. Since the exclusive design convinced the Albertina Passage as well as the guests who come there, it is now produced by TON and can be bought for private use in the living or dining room.

Photography by TON

Clip Daybed
Utopus studio

Designer	Javier Robles
Dimensions	H63 x W183 x D107cm
Materials	Steel frame, stainless steel legs and fittings, felt upholstery

The Clip Daybed was conceived as a piece of furniture with removable side arms and frames, which gives the body many seating and resting configurations and can be displayed and used in functions such as work, play and relaxation, as well as sleep. The removable stainless steel tube frame provides support for the two round side pillows, while the round section cushions provide arm and neck support, giving the design a playful and utilitarian configuration.

Photography by Utopus studio

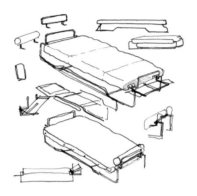

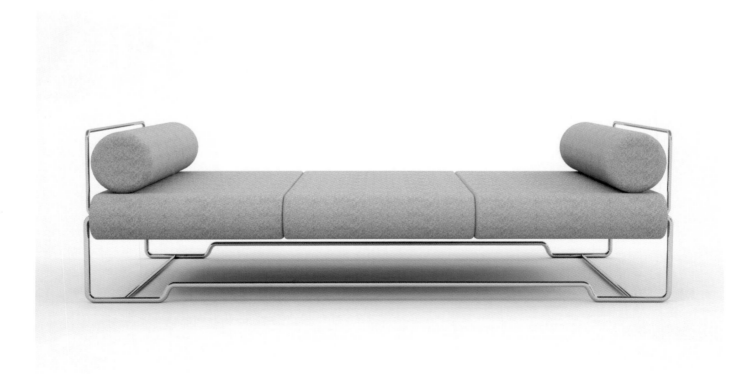

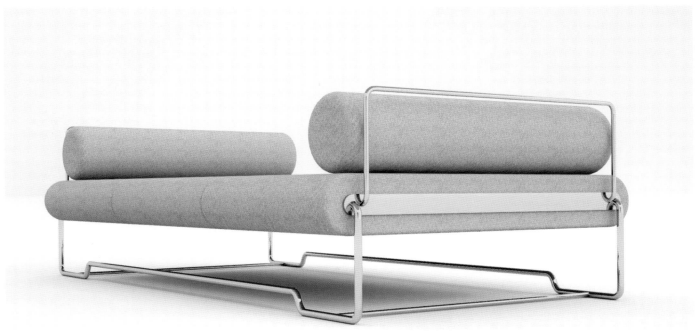

Coffee Table and End Table
Griffin Enright Architects

This custom coffee table features an asymmetrical, powder-coated, cantilevered steel frame with a 18mm-thick glass top and wood box for storage. The wooden box, with a drawer for storage, also floats beneath the plane of glass as it is discretely attached to the bottom of the frame. Along with the coffee table is an end table composed of the complementary material palette. The frame is also powder-coated steel, but the top comprises two translucent resin panels sandwiching the upper portion of the frame to create a glowing slot of space. The panels have a sanded finish and are embedded with seagrass that creates a layered texture with the doubling of the panels.

Photography by Margaret Griffin

Dimensions   Coffee table L122 x W76 x H43cm
              End table L76 x W76 x H76cm

Materials   Coffee table 2cm powder-coated steel tube frame,
              18mm tempered glass, birch drawer
              End table 2cm powder-coated steel tube frame,
              16mm resin top with seagrass

Convertible Island
workshop/apd

Tables come in many shapes and sizes for many different types of functions. This kitchen island functions both as a dining table, at standard dining table height, and as an auxiliary prep table, at kitchen counter height. The raised portion rolls on castors and can be stationed in any position along the length of the table. The materials are simple and practical – a Corian surface for food preparation and a glass surface for dining, all accented by a supple and organic live-edge walnut base. It is available in several sizes and finishes.

Photography by Donna Dotan Photography

Design team	Andrew Kotchen, Matthew Berman, J. Tyler Marshall
Dimensions	Counter: H91 x W91 x D86cm Tabletop: H76 x W61 x D305cm
Materials	Corian counter, glass tabletop, walnut base

Custom Sink
Griffin Enright Architects

Custom concrete countertops and sinks work with the palette of modern bathrooms to become sculptural elements within the space. They float above the ground plane like an elevated slab, with a seamless carved-out depression for the sink. The architect incorporated a cut in the front of the piece to create a slot for the hand-towel. The cohesive approach eliminates the need for an additional off-the-shelf towel holder. The floating sink becomes like a piece of sculpture – the modern geometry and a language of rectilinear slots and holes define it perfectly, while the material aggregate in the moulded concrete gives the sinks a monolithic and stone-like feel.

Photography by Benny Chan Fotoworks

Dimensions	W274 x D56 x H13cm
Materials	Custom cast-in-place concrete, alabaster

Dimensions   W117 x D48 x H13cm

Materials   Custom cast-in-place concrete, white veneer

D-LINE Desk

Philip Michael Wolfson

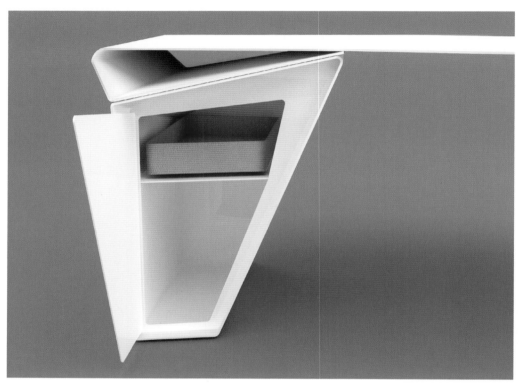

With the D-LINE – D is short for dynamic – series, Philip Michael Wolfson examines the dialogue of angle and circle, line and plane, and the resulting geometric distortion and motion. Relevant to each piece is the creation of a canvas of static versus dynamic forces, examining void and materiality, which rhythmically plays with shaping space and the manner in which it is discerned.

D-LINE pieces are concrete representations of movement along a continuous dynamic orbit. Geometric forms and shapes outlining a trajectory – a sphere of influence – both actual and perceived, engage both our linear and peripheral vision, to give an impression of the object (fixed) and the object in motion as one construct – a captured moment in time.

There is a vital equilibrium established that stimulates a desire to distinguish subtle differences and degrees of balance/imbalance. This forcefulness in the asymmetry creates what can be seen as an equilibrium of maximum strength and harmony. Through a minimalist simplicity, and a distortion of the geometry, through a pure and still whiteness, the mind continues to draw the line where it has physically ended.

Photography by Maxim Nilov

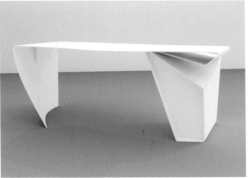

Dimensions   H75 x L180 x D95cm

Material   Painted carbon steel desk;
leather tray

Dining Table and Chair
Marmol Radziner

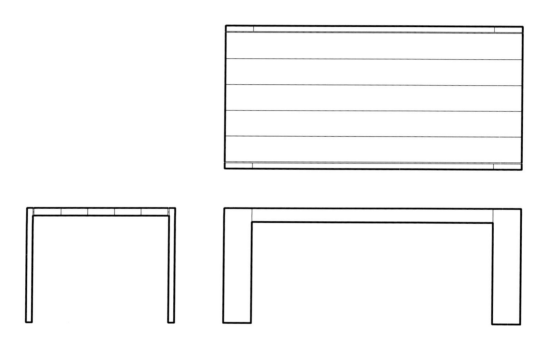

Dimensions | H74 x D91 x W244cm
Materials | Solid walnut or maple, blackened or stainless steel

Marmol Radziner Furniture is a natural extension of Marmol Radziner, a unique design/build firm known for its careful attention to detail and finish. Designed and built by architects, Marmol Radziner Furniture is created in-house in the firm's cabinet and metal shops, producing a line of furniture with clarity of design and integrity of construction.

Over the years, single pieces for individual clients had been produced, but the opportunity to design a full furniture collection in 2001 arose with a commission for a private residence. Growing directly out of the design and in line with the same principles of the house, Marmol Radziner developed and fabricated the furniture. Stressing proportions, lack of ornamentation, and an emphasis on how materials connect, both the house and furniture become one with the total design.

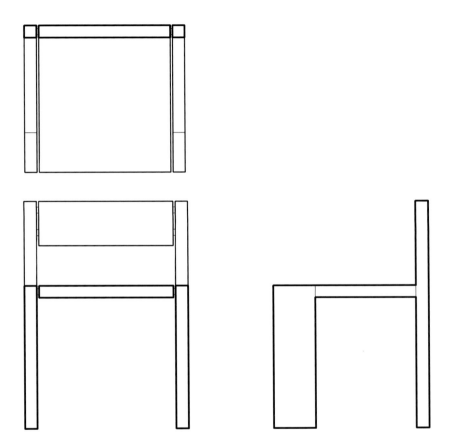

Composed of rich materials such as stainless and blackened steel, teak, walnut and plush fabrics, the Marmol Radziner Furniture collection includes the Dining, Living, Bedroom, Indoor/Outdoor, Vienna Way, Ranch, and Kings Road Groups. The Dining Group is grounded in rich maple and walnut, with clean lines and solid construction. The wood finish is emphasised with expansive surfaces and broad vertical planes. Wide table and chair legs lend weight and stature, creating a formal and unified collection. The pieces embrace the Modernist idiom of clean lines and simple forms, balancing textures and materials with the same precision and attention to detail given to the firm's architectural projects.

Photography by Benny Chan Fotoworks

Dimensions   H71 x D47 x W50cm

Materials   Solid walnut or maple,
leather upholstery,
blackened or
stainless steel

Dove Stool
design brian steendyk

Dove is the inspired sculptural expression of the beauty and movement of a bird, wings swept back, about to take flight. The stackable Dove metal stool is also informed by the fast pace of modern life, with little time to rest and recline. Dove's versatility brings a sense of grace to life and can be sat on from different directions, stacked quickly, and moved at a moment's notice. Quick, convenient and dynamic, Dove wire stools come in a variety of heights, including 44cm and 77cm, ideal for the residential environment, as well as a café or bar setting. Dove is flight captured in a chair.

Photography by Brian Steendyk and Christopher Frederick Jones

Dimensions   H44/77 x W42 x D37cm (small/large)
Material   Wire

Entelechy Series II: Lounge Chair
John Portman & Associates

Designer	John C. Portman
Dimensions	H84 x D107 x W79cm
Materials	Black leather, stainless steel frame

When John Portman decided he wanted to design furniture, he was inspired by the Barcelona Chair, not because it was a chair, but because it was timeless, and looks as good today as it did when it was designed in 1929. So he set out to design furniture that would stand the test of time. With each piece, he focused on balancing aesthetics and comfort in the conception of something organically unique. From the elegance of the materials chosen to the design itself, his goal was always to create furniture that was functional, comfortable, timeless and distinct.

A Portman chair is more than something upon which to sit. Humans can sit anywhere. They can sit on the ground, or on a rock. They can perch on a ledge. Why do they want a chair? What do they want from that chair? When will this particular chair be used? What setting will it be responding to? All these factors are considered and twined together to become a functional, comfortable, distinct chair. The elegant Entelechy Lounge Chair is light, comfortable and easy to move. It fits the human body and offers support when it's time to rise, and is an elegant work of art in and of itself.

Photography by Haigwood Studios

Flakes Chair 2.0
schmidt hammer lassen design

The classic and popular Flakes chair by the Finnish manufacturer, Piiroinen, has now been launched in a new 2.0 version. It has the same simple and timeless design as the original handmade glass-fibre version from 2005, but is now injection-moulded recyclable polypropylene. The design has been slightly scaled up to give added back support and comfort, particularly important for applications such as studying or sitting around a dining table. The scaled-up seat provides superb backrest support without compromising the simplicity and ease in which it can be handled. Furthermore, the added acoustic properties of polypropylene, as a material, add value to the interior space by giving a soft and pleasant sound.

Photography by Piiroinen

350 mm

470 mm

580 mm

580 mm

540 mm

1:10

Dimensions	H47/82 (seat/back) x W54 x D58cm
Materials	Chrome-plated steel tube, polypropylene seat
Colours	White, black, dark brown, light grey, dark grey, red, cream

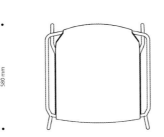

FLO Light

Foster + Partners in collaboration with Lumina

Dimensions   Range from H36–110cm

Materials   Aluminium frame, steel base, 6W LED

The FLO range of lights is the result of Foster + Partners' first collaboration with specialist Italian lighting manufacturer, Lumina. Available as a floor or desk lamp, the minimal light integrates the latest dimmable LED technology within a streamlined, curving form. The cold-formed head and slender aluminium frame are balanced by a circular steel base and a delicate profile is created by eliminating superfluous moving parts, such as coils and springs. The head can also be rotated by 300 degrees for direct task lighting. FLO provides 475 lumens from a 6-watt LED and, for future flexibility, the citizen LED module is interchangeable and can be easily upgraded.

Photography by Lumina

Floor Lamp
Base Architecture

Shawn Godwin originally created the lamp to display in the annual Base Exhibition, the theme influencing this innovation being 'Old & New'. The lamp was displayed along with the following descriptive text, "Balance of light: Tectonics and materials align themselves to assist the function of light and become one. New, old, salvaged, rough and refined collaborate to produce an everyday necessity".

Elements of the adjustable floor lamp including the timber stand were crafted from salvaged material epitomising the 'old' component, while the lamp's teardrop light fixture and off-form concrete base contrasts as the 'new', refined and rough factor, respectively. The floor lamp weighs a generous 25kg, stands at 214cm tall and the arm extends 120cm with an adjustable function to change the angle with which it outreaches.

Photography by Christopher Frederick Jones

Dimensions	H214cm; Arm extends to 120cm
Materials	Salvaged timber, off-form concrete, silver teardrop lighting fixture

 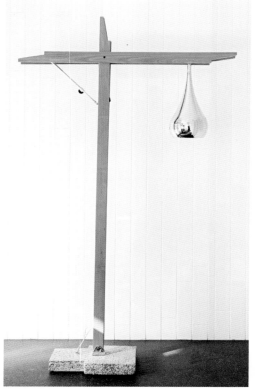 

Flotsam and Jetsam Table
Marcus O'Reilly Architects

The Flotsam and Jetsam series evolved after architect Marcus O'Reilly decided to turn some appealing pieces of driftwood he had found washed up on the beach near his home in Melbourne into a piece of furniture. After incorporating the driftwood into a coffee table, more furniture and commissions followed, adding to the Flotsam and Jetsam range.

The driftwood components were gathered on beaches near and far. Pieces that show some evidence of their past life – for instance, parts of boats, stampings, weathered paint layers, among others – were selected first and foremost. As the series developed, pieces were sourced on overseas and local trips. The driftwood was then sanded, shaped, cut to size, and in some cases a touch of colour was added; then the pieces were fixed to a black zinc steel frame.

The Flotsam and Jetsam coffee tables can be 'flat packed' which, in a lovely twist, allows the driftwood, which has arrived quietly by sea, to be airfreighted back to a new home. To date, tables have been flown to Italy, Switzerland and Kuwait, as well as being sent all around Australia.

Photography by Dianna Snape

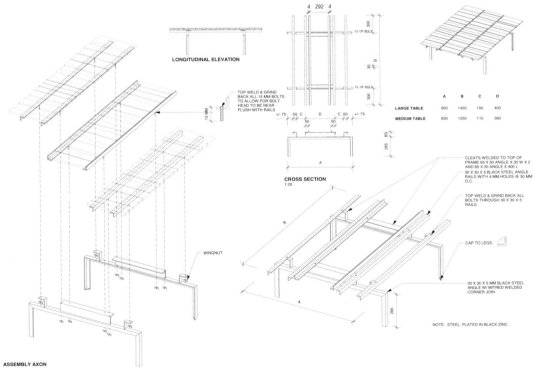

LONGITUDINAL ELEVATION

4   292   4

CL OF BOLT

300

30

B

300

CL OF BOLT

TOP WELD & GRIND
BACK ALL 15 MM BOLTS
TO ALLOW FOR BOLT
HEAD TO BE NEAR
FLUSH WITH RAILS

15 MM

	A	B	C	D
LARGE TABLE	950	1450	150	400
MEDIUM TABLE	830	1250	110	360

+/- 75   50 C   D   C 50   +/- 75
50   50

85

285

A

CROSS SECTION
1:20

WINGNUT

CLEATS WELDED TO TOP OF
FRAME 65 X 50 ANGLE X 30 W X 2
AND 65 X 50 ANGLE X 400 L
30 X 30 X 5 BLACK STEEL ANGLE
RAILS WITH 4 MM HOLES @ 30 MM
O.C.

TOP WELD & GRIND BACK ALL
BOLTS THROUGH 30 X 30 X 5
RAILS

B

CAP TO LEGS

A

285

30 X 30 X 5 MM BLACK STEEL
ANGLE W/ MITRED WELDED
CORNER JOIN

NOTE: STEEL PLATED IN BLACK ZINC.

ASSEMBLY AXON

Designer   Marcus O'Reilly
Dimensions   H40 x L150 x W83cm
Materials   Recovered driftwood,
                zinc steel frame

Fonda Bench
Techne Architects

Materials   Black steel frame, 6mm horse
halter rope by CH Smith Marine

In designing the fit-out for a Mexican restaurant in Melbourne, there was an opportunity to integrate the design of some special custom furniture and lighting pieces. Techne Architects always value the benefit that this bespoke work can give to the client and their project. In this case the built-in rope-strung bench seats reflect traditional Mexican craft and respond to the linear and angular approach taken throughout. They also complement the 'Acapulco Chair'-inspired light fittings that were designed for the space. The bench seats are constructed of black powder-coated steel tubular frame, which has an interlocking detail with the adjoining seat. The back is formed by lashing the framing with multi-coloured rope, which remains in tension. The overall design effect is light, utilitarian and subtly vibrant and playful.

Photography courtesy of the designer

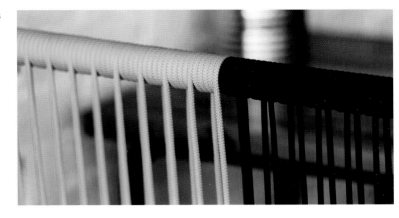

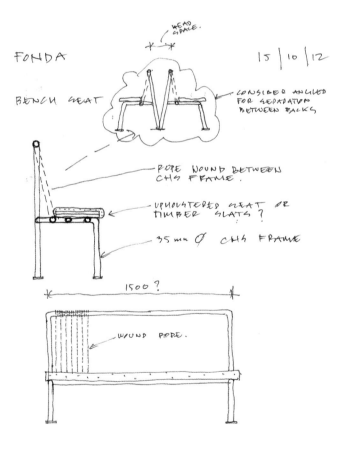

FOSS Pendant Light
FINNE Architects

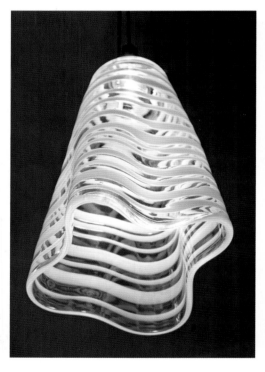

The pendant light fixture measures about 25cm high and is made from handblown glass, stainless cable and a brushed nickel lampholder. The fixture's freeform shape evokes the flow of water, and the fixture's name, FOSS, is the Norwegian word for waterfall. The MR-16 or LED lamp is located above the glass shade in order to evenly illuminate the handblown glass. The fixture takes the more standard pendant configuration – lamp inside shade – and turns it inside out.

Photography by Benjamin Benschneider

Design	Nils Finne
Dimensions	H25cm, diameter 12cm
Materials	Handblown glass, brushed nickel

Foster 520 Armchair for Walter Knoll

Foster + Partners

Dimensions	H42/96 (seat/back) x W72 x D95cm
Materials	Saddle leather exterior, soft upholstered interior

The Foster 520 armchair follows a series of successful collaborations with Walter Knoll and is the first in a new family of chairs developed specifically for manufacture, rather than for a particular project – already, the chair has won a coveted 'best of the best' Red Dot Design Award. Drawing on both traditional craft techniques and modern production methods, the high-backed leather armchair is designed to suit a variety of office or residential settings.

The armchair is based on three flat patterns, which are cut from leather and stitched together to create a single, flowing piece of furniture with the minimum number of surfaces. Its form derives from ergonomic studies and a series of prototypes, and the refined linear profile is designed to visually reduce the chair's bulk.

Offering the texture and comfort of a traditional leather armchair, the outer shell is made of tough saddle leather, with a contrasting soft upholstered interior. The two elements are connected by a visible stitch, which follows the line of the chair like the sweep of a hand-drawn sketch. The chair can be customised in a variety of colours, materials and combinations and it comes with a separate footstool.

Photography by Nigel Young

Foster 550 LED Lights

Foster + Partners with Louis Poulsen

Dimensions	Diameter 55cm, H4cm
Materials	Opal glass shade, matt anodised aluminium reflector, metalised polycarbonate light guide, aluminium ring, 7W LEDs
Colours	White, grey, aluminium

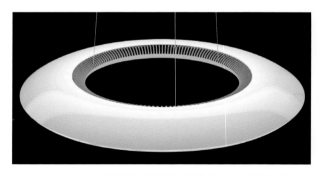

Foster 550 is the first in a range of light fittings and the result of an exciting collaboration between Louis Poulsen and Foster + Partners. The light challenges the idea that using a large number of LEDs must lead to bulky, oversized fittings, and surpasses the technical limitations of its components to achieve discreet lighting. Initially designed as a commercial product, it also has potential for residential applications.

The family of objects that comprises the 'kit of parts' lighting system is versatile, rising to the challenges presented by both interior and exterior demands to create a seamless transition between the two. The central aim during the design process was to achieve the right incandescent effects, rather than to visually demonstrate the technology. For this reason, the LED bulbs are discreetly hidden from view. This also allows for the light source to be replaced, as future LED improvements are made over time. Pared down to function and elegant form, the lumière deals efficiently with the limitations of the technology – the beauty of the design resting with the light source – expressed simply by the transference of light.

Photography by Nigel Young

Freestanding Ashtrays
Utopus studio

Design team	Javier Robles, Erik Weiss
Dimensions	Fin: H76 x W15 x D15cm
	The Number One: H76 x W18 x D18cm
Materials	Hammered polished chrome, walnut, glass, natural stone

Fin Ashtray

This freestanding ashtray was designed as an accessory that can be moved around in different social smoking areas. A black marble slab anchors the chrome pole, which supports the rounded textured ashtray, while the stained oak wood handle allows for a comfortable grip when moving the ashtray to the user's desired location and orientation.

Photography by Hai Zhang

The Number One Ashtray

This model was designed as a cigar ashtray to be used while the smoker is in the seated position. Ribbons of polished chrome support a makassar ashtray, creating a minimal profile when viewed from the side. The base of the stand houses a solid block of stone, resulting in an even, low centre of gravity, helping to support the ashtray to stay upright.

Photography by Hai Zhang

Gleam Shelving
Holt Clifford Designers

The notion of commercial metal adjustable shelving is a much-maligned area. The term 'adjustable shelving' gives rise to images of beige library interiors and dimly lit storerooms in back offices. Possibly unsettling, as they remind us of the drudgery of work, the archives representing a stultifying lack of esprit or deeper psychological archiving.

On the other hand, the way commercial industrial objects are made was at once earnestly and joyfully explored by contemporary artists including Donald Judd, Liam Gillick and Dan Flavin. There is so much seduction in the images and objects, but these objects easily support the weight of ideas and histories placed upon them by artistic activity.

The Gleam shelving system was devised as a celebration of the delight in the monotony and repetition of manufacturing, reduced to its simplest forms, and the exuberance and creativity that the aforementioned and many other artists see in the materials gleaned from industrial manufacture.

Gleam is a one-size shelf set into a 50mm pitch track. It has been devised to ensure a space between the side bracing walls to exploit the enthusiastic use of colour. The fuller the shelves, the more randomly placed, and the more the quiet riot ensues.

The 3mm-thick aluminium walls are rendered in an array of richly nuanced colours using a high micron anodising process normally used on building façades. This finish is extremely scratch-resistant for an anodised aluminium surface and has the benefit of beautifully saturated colour. Gleam elevates the mundane, yet supports the wildest of ideas through a subtle shift in proportion and finish.

Photography by Pia Photo, Donald Holt, Trevor Mein and JP Sante

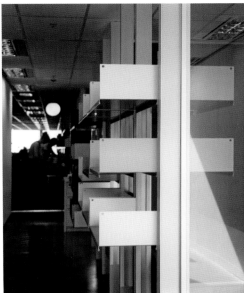

Dimensions	Shelf: W80 x D30 x H22cm, with 5cm pitch
	Wall strip: W150 x D100 x H50cm, with 5cm pitch
Materials	Aluminium with exterior grade anodising
Colours	Natural, dirt bronze, green, citron, baby pink, blue black, red clay

Grandstand Outdoor Table
Push Architects

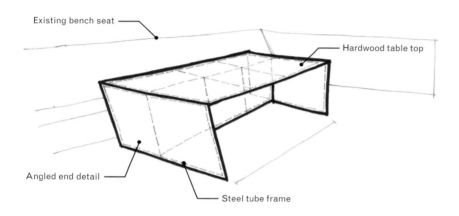

Existing bench seat

Hardwood table top

Angled end detail

Steel tube frame

The Grandstand Outdoor Table was designed to complement the outdoor entertainment area of the Grandstand House, an award-winning design recognised in the RAIA Queensland Architecture Awards 2009.

The angled end detail is a feature of the table, which was inspired by the existing corner of the house and adjacent bench seat. The table has an ironbark hardwood tabletop supported by a steel tube frame. With a brief to enable large groups to sit comfortably, utilising the built-in deck bench seat and accommodate loose chairs, it was designed for solidity and sturdiness, as it is on display to the street.

Photography by Michael Chen

Design team	Paul Curran
Dimensions	H78 x L285 x W124cm
Material	Ironbark hardwood top, steel tube frame

Holey Tree
Cullinan Ivanov Architects

Design   **Vladimir Ivanov**
Manufacturer   **Camp Cove Creative**
Materials   **Birch plywood**

Architect Vladimir Ivanov always found the idea of chopping a beautiful young tree for just two weeks at Christmas time a terrible waste, compounded by the sight of dead yellow trees lying on the kerb in January, waiting to be picked up by the next garbage collection. So when his son Pavel was born, he knew that he had to do something about Christmas. Frustrated with the uninspiring alternatives on the market, Ivanov set about designing a tree that was long-lasting, inspiring, beautiful and a little more environmentally friendly. Living in a terrace, it also had to be easy to store. The result was the Holey Tree, a modern take on the traditional Christmas tree.

It is a contemporary, exquisitely shaped piece that can look elegant in any house, apartment or in the office. The tree consists of just three parts, which slot together, and can be neatly flat-packed away under the bed or in the cupboard after the festive season. The tree is made from the highest quality birch plywood, which is sustainable, renewable and durable. It is CNC-cut, which also allows for the most economical use of the plywood sheet. The cut-outs in the tree allow for the hanging of existing decorations. Or better still, family and friends can be creative and make some custom decorations for it each year, giving the tree its own unique character.

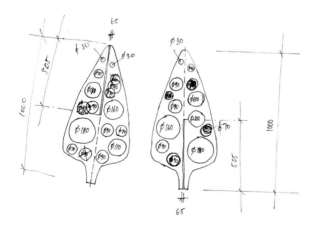

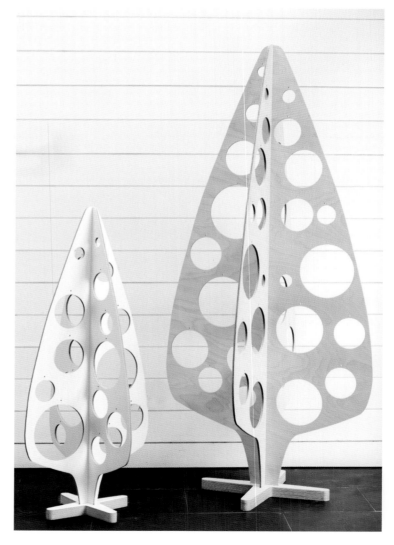

Honeycomb Gardening System

STUDIOTJOA

This modular stacking system consists of modular units that can be combined in numerous variations to suit the user's needs. The planter cups fit within the latticework of the honeycomb and holds soil for the growing of plants, vegetables and herbs. The storage tube keeps gardening tools out of the way but close to the plants and can also be used to house new seedlings. The cap fits both the storage tube and the planter to protect the new seedlings, should the weather suddenly turn cold. The caps can also be used alone in the honeycomb structure to create a surface, if necessary. The honeycomb structure disassembles for shipping and when assembled, multiple units can stack or sit next to each other to create a usable piece of furniture for a patio or inside the home.

Photography and renderings by Audrey Worden and Alexander Worden

Design team   Audrey Worden,
Alexander Worden
Dimension   H46 x W46 x D46cm
Materials   Aluminium,
translucent resin

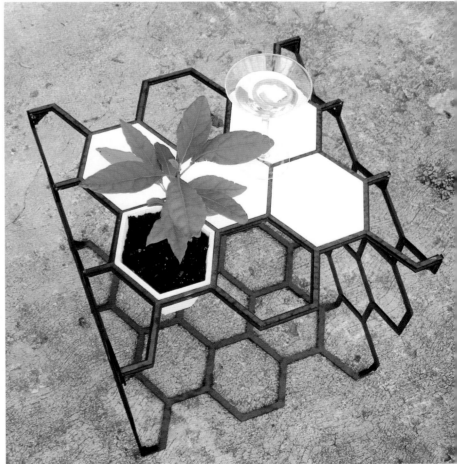

Hudson Panos Table
Swatt | Miers Architects

Designer	Robert Swatt
Dimensions	H75 x L249 x W110cm
Materials	White oak or walnut, brushed stainless steel plate

Most of Swatt | Miers' furniture designs are based on simple structural ideas. In the Hudson Panos Table, thick wood slabs cantilever over linear wood beams and supporting wood slab legs. Tension is added to the composition by splitting the table longitudinally, creating two half-tables separated by a 5cm void. Stainless steel plates located halfway up the slab legs connect the two halves, creating the appearance of a single unit. Because the house features Western Red Cedar siding and Douglas fir exposed beams, a rich, deep, solid walnut was selected in order to provide contrast.

Photography by Russell Abraham and Robert Swatt

Iceberg Nightstand
workshop/apd

In an exploration of geometry, workshop/apd created a wall-hung nightstand that is unconventional in form. Inspired by cut crystals and the facets of gemstones, this furniture accent automatically cools down a space, giving it a modern and refreshed look. The nightstand exterior is constructed with a white lacquer finish and a maple interior. This piece is wall-mounted with one drawer and also comes in custom sizes and finishes.

Photography by T. G. Olcott

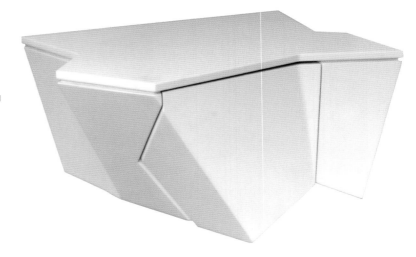

Design team	Andrew Kotchen, Matthew Berman, Leslie Degler
Dimensions	H23 x W43 x D30cm
Materials	White lacquer exterior, clear maple interior

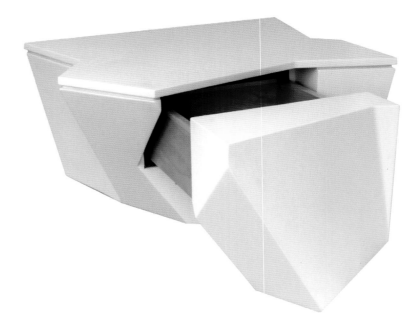

IXI Hanging Light
Filippo Caprioglio – Caprioglio Associati Studio di Archittetura

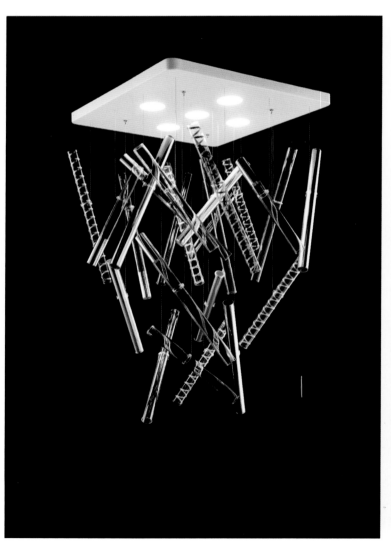

The concept behind the IXI hanging light comes from the idea of a democratic design intended to give anybody the possibility of conceiving the setting of each single glass piece and to compose the chandelier according to personal taste. An initial design is chosen from a selection of 24 differently finished pieces. The design features individual glass rods with reflective metallic decorative elements that can be used for general illumination in various possible settings in a house or other multi-purpose space. Some of the tubes are mirrored to add to the reflectivity of the light that comes from above.

The idea of detaching the light-source from the decorative element allows for multiple and varied configurations. The energy-efficient LED light-source is concealed in a white lacquered, square metal ceiling canopy. The design can also be used to create room dividers or feature walls. In 2011 Caprioglio received the prestigious Good Design Award from The Chicago Athenaeum for this piece.

Photography by Claim Agency

Designer	Filippo Caprioglio
Manufacturer	Leucos – Murano Due
Dimensions	Diameter 65cm; maximum suspension from ceiling 120cm
Materials	Light: glass, crystal, mirror Ceiling canopy: lacquered metal
Weight	16.8kg
Bulbs	5 x 13W LED

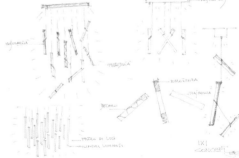

Jake Tables

Holt Clifford Designers

Round tables, rectangular tables, oval tables – is that all there is? The Jake table project began as a study of table shapes and sizes and how people react and relate to each other in these different proximities.

A deeper challenge developed when the designers looked for a universal system to support the eccentric tabletop shapes provided by the research. The result was both mundane and edgy. It was familiar, industry-ready and visually exciting.

The universal segmented base concept has been designed and in production since the 1960s. A post with cast elements allows various leg lengths and assemblies. The exception here was that the top shapes are not always universally symmetrical. What to do? Develop a quick system that can be fitted to the desired top shape in a unique yet repeatable way. In effect, this hit the core of mass customisation.

This was achieved by engineering an interlocking steel plate section that had maximum lightness and spread. It could be made as a one-off or highly repeatable at low cost. All the expensive and difficult-to-produce parts were the same across the system: a cast-aluminium knuckle, the post system and top fixing plates. The universal integral adjustable foot was developed to mitigate uneven floors.

The product was released in head-to-toe orange or white. Although it is now only offered in white and charcoal, the designers are itching to release it in a new block colour. So teal, emerald, cobalt and saffron may see the light of day.

Photography by Mark Ashkanasy and Kaz Morihata

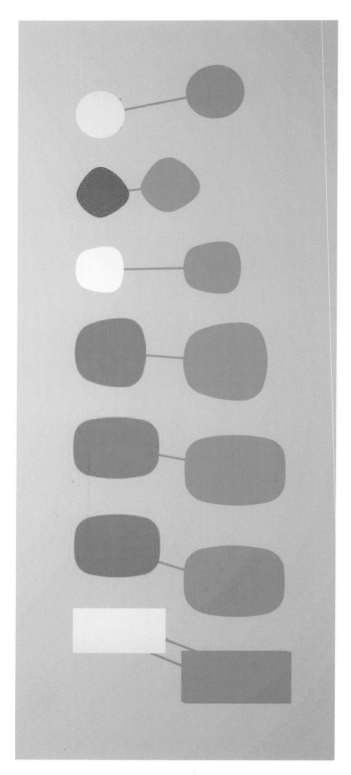

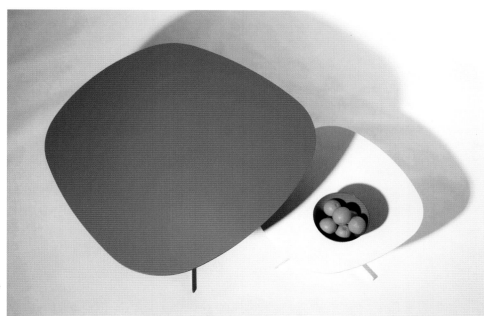

Dimensions H45/73/95cm, top in various sizes
Materials   Lacquered MDF top, cast
             aluminium, mild steel base,
             powder-coated silicon feet
Colours   White, charcoal, jeep green,
             orange

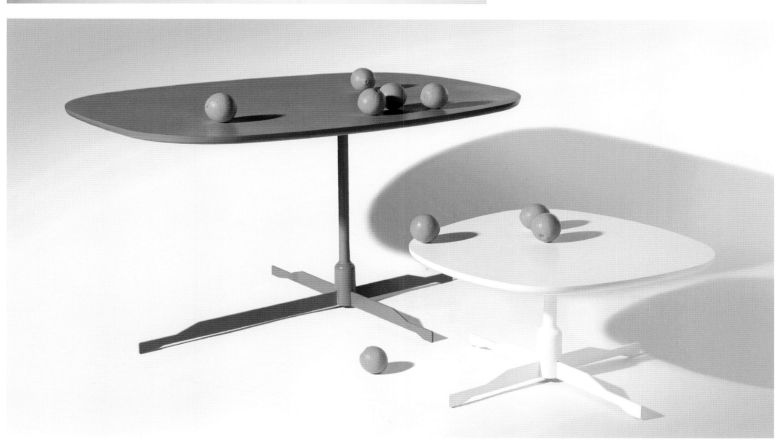

Light Boxes

Griffin Enright Architects

Dimensions W51 x L315 x D15cm,
W61 x L221 x D15cm (p.108, right),
W203 x L909 x D203cm (p.109, right)

Materials .6mm eco-resin panels, custom
steel tube frame, dimmable
3,000-kelvin fluorescent light

These custom light boxes, integrated into the ceiling-scape of residential projects, are a unique way to provide a glowing light for the main living spaces. They are constructed from 3-form panels, made of eco-resin with embedded seagrass, creating a soft, glowing and filtered lighting effect. The panels are attached to a custom steel frame that contains dimmable, fluorescent, 3,000-kelvin lights. This solution is functionally and compositionally beautiful, as an unexpected element within the landscape of the ceiling. They function to provide a different type of light in the space that works with less diffuse light to provide a layered lighting solution. The boxes break up the plane of the ceiling to create variation in colour and texture, as well as in relief. The light boxes are oriented to provide visual connections between the interior and exterior in each home, as well as to give cues for the narrative movement through the space.

Photography by Benny Chan Fotoworks

Liquid Glacial Dining & Coffee Table
Zaha Hadid Design

The Liquid Glacial design embeds surface complexity and refraction within a powerful fluid dynamic. The elementary geometry of the flat tabletop appears transformed from static to fluid by the subtle waves and ripples evident below the surface, while the table's legs seem to pour from the horizontal in an intense vortex of water frozen in time. The transparent acrylic material amplifies this perception, adding depth and complexity through a flawless display of infinite kaleidoscopic refractions. The result generates a wonderful surface dynamic that inherits a myriad of colours from its context and continually adapts with the observer's changing viewpoint. The form is of its creator, a design that does not compromise functionality or ergonomic requirements and a coherent evolution of her architectural narrative exploring movement through space.

Photography by Jacopo Spilimbergo

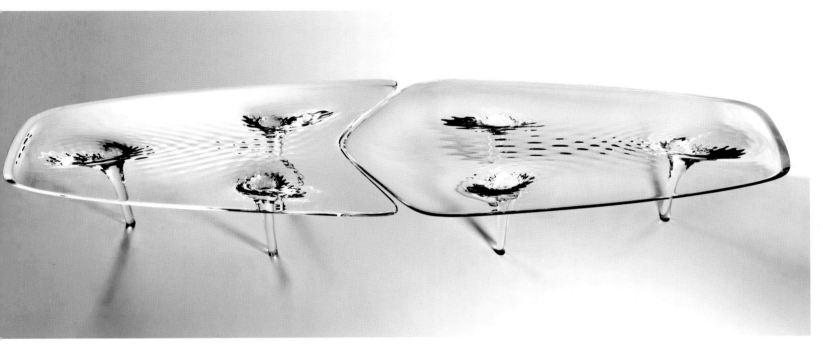

Design	Zaha Hadid, Patrik Schumacher
Design Team	Fulvio Wirz, Mariagrazia Lanza, Maha Kutay, Woody Yao
Dimensions	Dining Table: Section 1 H75 x L252 x D140cm, Section 2 H75 x L283 x D141cm
	Coffee Table: L250 x D87 x H40cm
Material	Polished clear Plexiglas

Little Giraffe

Holt Clifford Designers

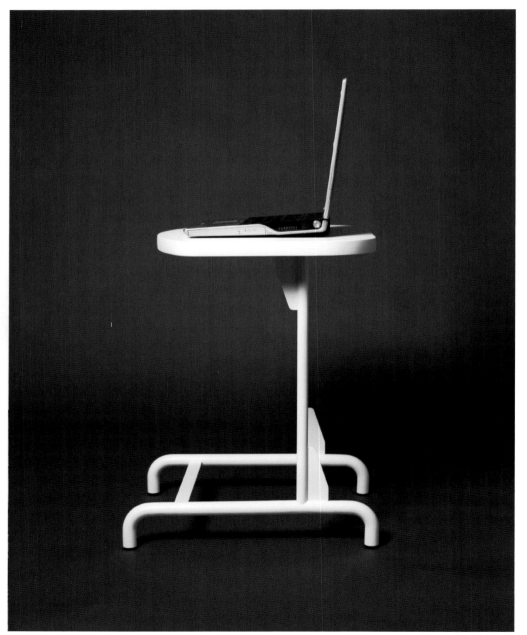

Dimensions	H60/80 (small/large) x W50 x D39cm
Materials	Lacquered MDF top, mild steel base, powder-coated nylon feet
Colours	White, black, safety yellow or custom colour

The Little Giraffe is a small table set at a height for laptop or casual meeting use. It can stretch its neck over a bench or sofa for easy use and is high enough to get the knees under comfortably. A higher version was developed for training rooms to set over demountable tables, without having to dislodge the technology.

It is made from laser-cut steel plate and rotationally laser-cut steel tube. The result is a small kit of pieces that click together for near effortless assembly and concealment of welds and fixings. The assembled steel is powder-coated and matching (and sometimes not) tops of a soft 'D' shape made from lacquered E0 MDF are fixed to the frame. Four nylon feet finish the object.

Detailed thinking about use, customisation and ease of ordering and assembly are key to the piece. This assembly focus informs the aesthetic but in turn the table's intentional awkwardness was born of the process and encouraged to project the unique feel and look of this table.

This product evolved from a specific relationship into a general usefulness. At its inception it was developed in conjunction with a small metal fabrication company to provide a piece of furniture that could be produced when the usual custom manufacturing was running a little slowly.

Photography by Pia Photo and JP Sante

Lo Glo Lights
J. MAYER H. Architecture Design Research

Lo Glo comprises piled-up discs that glow in the dark – elastic forms that gently yield and deform as we use them. It is possible to talk about the interactive or performative surfaces of J. MAYER H., and how they activate experience, including this most recent, unprecedented stage of research into the scale of furniture. And it is possible to recall how this interactivity, however physical, is also phantasmagoric, and operates firmly within the realm of the remembered, the uncanny, and the longed for. Jürgen Mayer makes things that touch back. His earlier, thermosensitive works depend on our caress; with 'LoGlo', Mayer ascribes a more autonomous inner life. These are works that hover in a quasi-subjective realm, greeting our bodies with an unmistakable stickiness. It is a pseudoscience Mayer pursues, with none of the heaviness of neo-Organicist claims. No biomimicry here. 'Lo Glo' is pure fiction: a cake that looks like a tree, spun and glazed like a dense and chewy story.

Photography by Thomas Dix for Vitra and
J. MAYER H Architecture Design Research

Design team   Jürgen Mayer H., Marcus Blum

Dimensions   Diameter varies from 56 to 118cm

Materials   Phosphorescent Nekrolon fabric

Lofot Table
FINNE Architects

The Lofot Table consists of two intertwining, sensuous planes of bent laminated mahogany, with a flush intersection in the middle of the table. Each plane is constructed with a series of bent 3mm (1/8 inch) thick strips of mahogany, and each plane swells in the middle, so it is wider in the middle than at the ends. The base of the table is composed of intertwining pieces of bent 12mm (½ inch) steel plate, with a blackened finish. The overall dimensions of the table are 102 x 244cm (40 x 96 inches).

Photography by Benjamin Benschneider

Design	Nils Finne
Manufacturer	Metalwork: ILLUME
	Woodwork: Seaboard Cabinet Company
Materials	Laminated mahogany, blackened steel

Lunar Sofa System

Utopus studio

This is a modular, low-profile sofa system
made for lounges and living rooms – a sectional
seating arrangement for a private residence.
The individual modules are made to express an
extruded form, allowing for a continuous length
of seating if modules are placed adjacently in
alignment. The 'ends' of the modules expose
a brightly coloured fabric as an accent to
the otherwise neutral palette.

Photography by Erik Weiss

Designer	Javier Robles
Dimensions	H41/76 (seat/back) x W107 x D107cm
Materials	Various upholstery materials, solid wood core

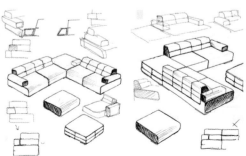

Mille-Feuille

emmanuelle moureaux architecture + design

Imagined as thin layers of coloured sheets scattered in the air, then settling randomly on top of each other, creating overhangs and recessions, the Mille-Feuille storage series, designed by Emmanuelle Moureaux and created by German furniture manufacturer Schonbuch was revealed at the Wallpaper Handmade Exhibition in Milan. Employing her signature use of colour, Emmanuelle draws inspiration from similar but larger-scale previous explorations, such as her Sugamo Shinkin Bank (Shimura Branch) project.

The colourful storage pieces are handmade from layers of lacquered MDF and come in three sizes: 21 layers for a multicoloured cabinet, 12 layers for a green-blue low cabinet and eight layers for a yellow-pink bedside cabinet, all containing 'hidden' drawers. The function of the 'Mille-Feuille' may change according to the numbers of layers and the concept can be developed for other functions, such as a low table or a shelf.

Photography by Schonbuch

Manufacturer   Schonbuch
Material   Lacquered MDF
Colour   Available in 19 colours and white

minuscule™ Chair

Fritz Hansen

Designer   Cecile Mainz

Dimensions   H41/73 (seat/back) x W63 x D56cm

Materials   Polypropylene shell upholstered with PUR foam,
              zinc connectors, glass-filled nylon base with four
              steel pins

Colour   Ochre, denim blue, grey, green, dark blue grey,
              rust orange, beige, dark ultramarine blue, blue
              grey, dark blue aubergine, aubergine, corn yellow

Innovation meets loving craftwork, Danish furniture traditions in dialogue with curious originality, and elegance and soft forms unite designer Cecilie Mainz's new minuscule™ furniture series, which embodies comfortable qualities that do not put limitations on the design's expression. This is a chair that beautifully follows the lines of Arne Jacobsen's curvy classics.

The minuscule™ chair comes fully upholstered in Remix fabric in 12 different designer selections, with an option of either light or dark grey for the back of the chair. The sculptural shell with natural leather piping creates a severe edge towards the inner shell, which curves downwards. The chair padding has been kept light and elegant. This reinforces the feeling of a chair that is both informal and stringent at the same time.

Photography courtesy of the designer

Modular Outdoor Seating
SLHO & Associates

Design Team   Douglas Ho, Kenneth Tsang
Materials   Fibre-glass steel frame,
              EPDM exterior

Plants know no boundary, and when faced with obstacles, they will force their way through, fusing with the surroundings, blending in harmoniously. This furniture system, constructed from modular units, has the same nature as the natural world, capable of embracing existing forms, forming a new layer of fabric and connecting the disjointed surroundings.

Each module is constructed with a fibre-glass steel inner frame, with the exterior finished in EPDM, a common recyclable material that is normally used for the flooring of a playground. Porous in nature, the material can drain water fast, and allows air to be trapped inside, which makes the piece more stable in terms of temperature: warmer to the touch in the winter, while cooling down more quickly in summer.

Unlike how most furniture is constructed these days, fabricated in a mechanical environment, the EPDM layer is hand-finished and each piece is unique. The architect's decision in choosing this material was with consideration to its performance as well as returning to the time when handmade craft still mattered. This is particularly important, especially at times when the economy is weak and people are out of work. Do we want more mass production? Or do we want products that have a better human touch?

The modules can exist as a single piece of furniture, but thanks to the angles and dimensions in which they were designed, when placed in a cluster, and fixed at different levels, there are endless possibilities in terms of configuration.

This is an attempt to look at how furniture can be adapted instead of usual benches, using a single module to form different type of seating arrangements as well as becoming back support, table tops, or even an outdoor obstacle course for children. The possibility is endless.

Photography by SLHO & Associates

Modular Seating
Behnisch Architekten

Furniture supports and inspires our activities within a particular space. Due to their form and function, items of furniture have a big influence on the way we behave in a room. They can encourage communication or provide a space for retreat. Together with Rolf Benz, Behnisch Architekten have developed a system of modular seating furniture for commercial or professional use, which puts the main focus on informal communication, and subsequently on people.

When designing the modular seating furniture, Behnisch Architekten placed particular importance on the use of natural, high-quality materials such as wood and leather, also with regard to the upholstery fabrics. More than that, this was one of the basic ideas that influenced the design from the very beginning. A visible wooden frame with firm padding and the upright, high seating position with low and high backs are just as much a part of the commercial furniture concept as are work surfaces and possibilities for depositing things as intermediate elements.

Using a simple modular connecting system, the furniture can be used as a single chair or as a sofa – making it possible to sit in a formal or a more familiar circle, with and without the perceived boundary created by armrests or surfaces for depositing things. Situational communication in a comfortable setting is the basis of the design concept.

Photography by David Matthiessen (page 126) and Rolf Benz (page 127)

Manufacturer	Rolf Benz
Dimensions	Armchair: H44/97 (seat/back) x W80 x D80cm
Materials	Solid wooden legs, frame and inner frame, coil spring unit, polyurethane foam covered with polyester fleece; optional leather armrests

MONI Shelves
Objects by Estudio Carme Pinós

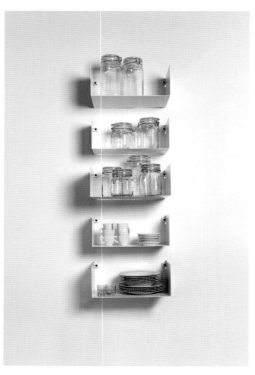

Designer	Carme Pinós
Dimensions	W38 x D20 x H16cm (MONI 20)
	W38 x D25 x H16cm (MONI 25)
	W38 x D30 x H16cm (MONI 30)
Material	2mm steel plate
Weight	2.15kg (MONI 20)
	2.7kg (MONI 25)
	3.25kg (MONI 30)
Colours	Dark grey coated steel with metallic effect, white coated steel, varnished black steel

A 2mm-thick folded piece of steel in a U-shape is the only material used to create a light, modular and resistant shelf. Subtle and made from simple lines, it adapts itself to any space and necessity, giving prominence to the objects it holds. It is the perfect solution for a library and it takes on a weightless appearance as the number of books grows. MONI is available in three different depths (20, 25 and 30cm) and finishes. The steel is cut by laser.

MYchair

UNStudio

Client	Walter Knoll
Design Team	Ben van Berkel, Martijn Prins, Christian Bergmann, Arne Nielsen
Sizes	H80 x D75.5 x W86.5cm
Materials	Chromed steel bar frame, foam seat upholstered with Trevira and Kvadrat fabrics or Walter Knoll leather

MYchair is the first chair designed by Ben van Berkel / UNStudio and is a real architect's chair. The architectural approach to furniture is different from that of the industrial designer: the architect begins with the space and the environment of which the chair will become a part. All the details of the chair, besides needing to be comfortable and fulfilling the normal functional requirements of a piece of furniture, are considered for their spatial effects. And, as each architect has his or her own understanding of the sort of space that they aim to generate, this architectural approach to furniture is intrinsically connected with a very personal ideology of space.

In the case of Ben van Berkel / UNStudio this spatial awareness is connected to his idea of the 'after image'. With this notion, Ben van Berkel refers to the capacity of three-dimensional objects to produce many different impressions when seen from different angles. These multiple views and continuously changing silhouettes result in a kaleidoscopic experience, achieved in the MYchair by the faceted arrangement of the soft elements, the inward and outward curves of the chrome frame and the duo-tones of the upholstering. All these elements are carefully orchestrated, which, in the theory of the architect, ultimately creates an 'after image' that is rich and stimulating, yet cohesive and balanced.

The way in which the idea of the after image is incorporated in the chair in such a unified manner is through the medium of reflection. Each detail is reflected in another. Thus, the facet shapes of the soft part of the chair are echoed in the curves of the frame supporting it; the bottom is reflected in the sides; and the room itself is reflected in the polished chrome of the support frame. Reflectiveness is also found in the details of the seat and the back support, which are arranged together to enable a variety of seating positions. In this way, legs tucked under, or turning sideways, the occupant of the chair engages in the spatial game envisaged by the architect, shifting positions and thereby shifting perspectives and images.

In the eighteen months or so that it took the architect to develop the design, many people passed the drawings and models of the chair dotted around the studio. Often, their response was, 'I'd like to have that chair. When is it ready?' The name MYchair reflects that response and its potential to appropriate, adapt, use and customise the chair in many ways, making it truly your own.

Photography by Bryan Adams

MYchair Lounge
UNStudio

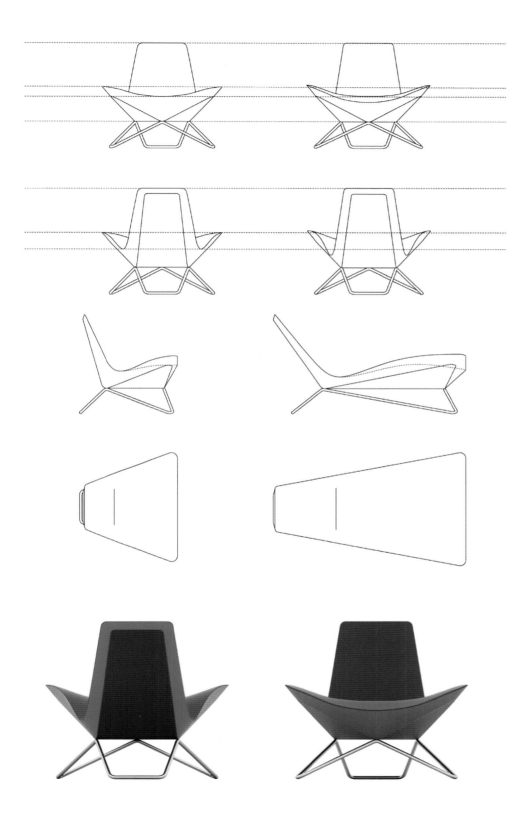

Extending Ben van Berkel's earlier MYchair into a family of related designs, MYchair Lounge was presented for the first time at the Walter Knoll stand in Milan in 2011. MYchair Lounge continues and extends the formal qualities and spatial effects of the earlier MYchair, with the facet shapes of the chaise longue-inspired seat echoed in the curves of the supporting frame.

Designer Ben van Berkel says, "MYchair Lounge is literally an expansion of the MYchair, both physically and conceptually. An actual stretching of the original chair extends the 'Coming Home' concept of relaxation and reflection even further".

Photography by Walter Knoll

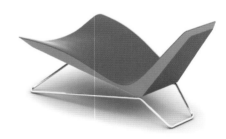

Client	Walter Knoll
Design Team	UNStudio: Ben van Berkel, Caroline Bos, Martijn Prins, William de Boer, Machteld Kors
	Walter Knoll: Markus Benz, Jürgen Rohm
Dimensions	H86 x L153 x W86cm
Materials	Chromed steel bar frame, foam seat upholstered with Tevira and Kvadrat fabrics or Walter Knoll leather

top

530

900

back

side

1510

834

48°

380

1328

front

480

200

bottom

922

1084

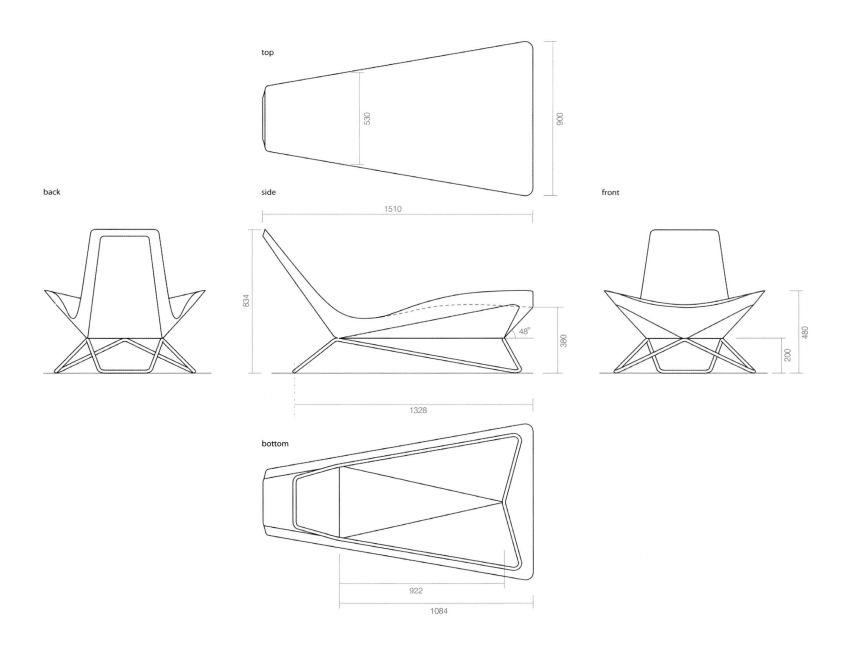

MYchair Lounge   **135**

Nichos

57STUDIO

Nichos is specially designed for limited spaces where many items need to be arranged in a confined space. It is designed for places where television is the centrepiece of the room – mainly master bedrooms and family rooms. The television niche in the centre can be connected to the stereo and any side equipment through the back, without cables being visible.

The depth created to incorporate the flat television allows the owner enough space to personalise their own Nichos, with individual niches to store DVDs, books, pictures and any other belongings they may wish to display.

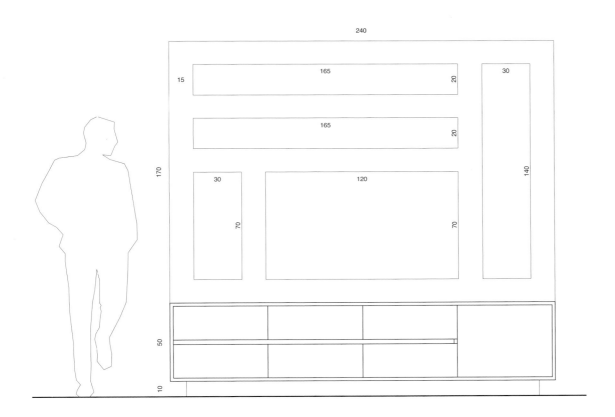

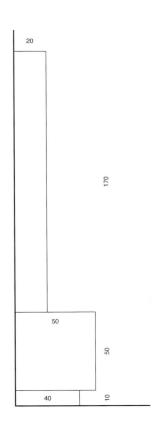

The base is much deeper than the top and is divided into four squared parts that can be designed at the owner's convenience. In the case of the piece featured opposite, the right side has been kept open to receive the equipment and six drawers have been incorporated in the other side.

Materials used are lacquered and wood-laminated MDF panels – satinated white and cedar in the illustrated example. The drawer handles are made from a special aluminium section designed by Häfele. The architect included a series of 10mm-thick glass shelves that can be organised according to personal preference.

Photography by Caco Oportot

Design team	Maurizio Angelini, Benjamín Oportot
Dimensions	H240 x W240 x D240cm
Materials	Wood-laminated MDF panels

Norfolk Table

WA Design, David Stark Wilson

Designer	David Stark Wilson
Dimensions	L244 x 107cm
Materials	Black lacquered quarter sawn oak legs, laminated glass top with embedded photographic image layer

For the Norfolk Table commission, the architect wanted to work with one cross-section of wood joined at 90-degree angles and let that simple concept become as eccentric, dynamic and complex as possible. He studied many configurations trying to emphasise the movement expressed by the strong diagonals, and wanted to abstract the table base into a sculpture that just happened to support a top. The functional requirement is met but in a newly imagined form.

Photography by David Stark Wilson

OTTA Table
FINNE Architects

Designer	Nils Finne
Dimensions	H40 x W81 x L86cm
Material	Blackened steel frame, clear and satin etch Starphire low-iron glass

This coffee table utilises an irregular blackened steel frame with
alternating panels of clear and satin etch Starphire low-iron glass.
The table explores the idea of abstracting natural forms and
fabricating them in a pure industrial material.

Photography by Benjamin Benschneider

Parenthetical Shelving

SsD architecture + urbanism

Beginning as a critique of vertically adjustable shelving where one has to remove all the materials to accommodate change, these shelves slide horizontally to instantly allow the co-existence of different-sized objects. The curved ends of each horizontal plane express the materiality of the bamboo plywood, as well as acting as bookends. Cantilevering the system from the wall creates an uncluttered and flexible storage and display system. Designed either for a person constantly rearranging their shelves or for multiple users who 'negotiate' the shelving space, the product brings a sense of whimsical play to a very practical problem.

The material used is sustainably harvested bamboo plywood that is mounted to horizontally sliding hardware. Approximately 2.1m wide, 40cm tall and 35cm deep, each shelf module can be installed separately or in a grouped set. Arrangements can span horizontally across a room, stack vertically, stagger or combine any of these configurations. Once fixed to the wall, even more options are possible through the movement of the units.

Part of the architect's larger concept of dynamic furniture, Parenthetical Shelving is one example in a line of furniture that supports evolutionary change, efficient use and multiple users. The architect believes that furniture should not limit lifestyles, but promote imagination and freedom.

Photography by SsD architecture + urbanism

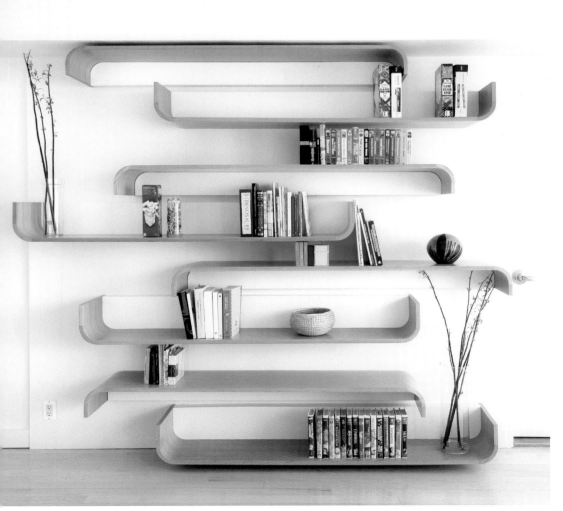

Design team	Jinhee Park, John Hong
Dimensions	W213 x H42 x D36cm
Material	Bamboo plywood

Prospect Outdoor Table

Push Architects

Designed to respond to the orientation and environment of the rooftop garden in which it sits, this table is elevated to take advantage of a view over the solid roof edge. The height is carefully considered in creating a top that is comfortable both to stand around or sit at on stools. A powder-coated steel frame forms the structure of the table, with ironbark hardwood slats forming the top. Loosely inspired by Japanese temple design, the structure is layered, articulated and simply exposed.

Photography by Michael Chen

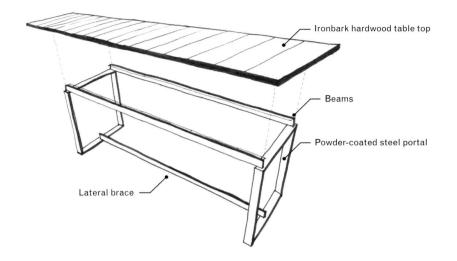

Ironbark hardwood table top

Beams

Powder-coated steel portal

Lateral brace

Design team | Paul Curran,
 | Annie Edwards
Dimensions | H90 x L240 x W90cm
Material | Ironbark hardwood
 | top, powder-coated
 | steel frame

Ro™ Chair
Fritz Hansen

Ro™ is the result of a close, two-year collaboration between the republic of Fritz Hansen and Jaime Hayon. Fritz Hansen's design brief for Jaime Hayon was to create a comfortable seat for one person. With this in mind, Jaime Hayon drew a series of sketches, which formed the start of the armchair's shape, expression and subsequent modelling work. Right from the start it was essential that the chair could provide a room within the room. It gives you the option of retreating and immersing yourself, while still remaining part of the surrounding room should you choose to.

The modelling work was conducted as an interaction between digital models and physical 1:1 styrofoam models. Physical models were made by hand and then digitalised. The digital files thus formed the basis of the millings, which were minutely crafted by hand and, after numerous repeats, the final Ro™ shape was born.

The legs in pressure-cast aluminium and the transition to the shell underwent the same process to create an elegant and natural unit, which ensures that Ro™ is beautiful and elegant from all angles. In order to make the chair more vivid and tactile, in addition to the shell's shape, a combination of different textiles were also employed – one for the shell and one for the cushions.

The material is sewn like a dress with just one seam, which follows the chair's edge exactly. Once the dress has been sewn, it is turned inside out and pulled on. Millimetre by millimetre it is glued on to the shell. Where the chair's body is narrow, there is excess material, and where the chair is wide, the material is stretched. This places enormous demands on both the material and the upholsterer. The materials and craftsmanship have been tested to the extreme.

Photography courtesy of the designer

Designer	Jaime Hayon
Dimensions	H61/113 (seat/back) x W80 x D97cm
Materials	Polyurethane shell, foam, brushed aluminium legs, nylon glides

Seating Stones
UNStudio

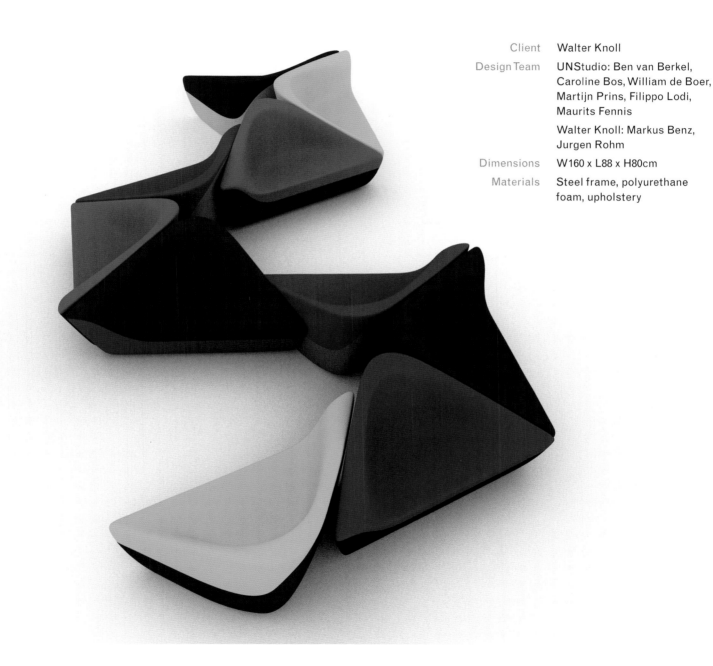

Client	Walter Knoll
Design Team	UNStudio: Ben van Berkel, Caroline Bos, William de Boer, Martijn Prins, Filippo Lodi, Maurits Fennis
	Walter Knoll: Markus Benz, Jurgen Rohm
Dimensions	W160 x L88 x H80cm
Materials	Steel frame, polyurethane foam, upholstery

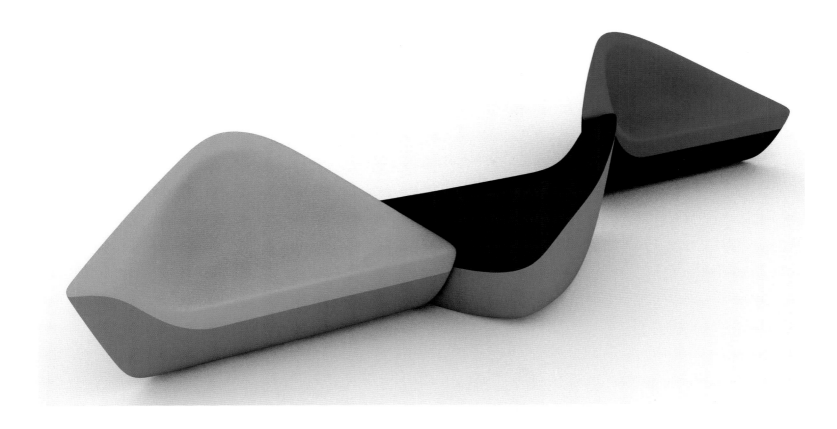

Throughout history, natural formations have been used to provide seating elements for rest, relaxation, gathering and communication. Inspired by the rhythmic smoothness of geological formations, the sculptural Seating Stones exhibit a playful take on spatial awareness and versatility, presenting myriad possibilities for placement, colour, texture, arrangement and communication.

Seating Stones are designed as individual objects and can be used autonomously. However, they can also be placed side by side as a family of forms in a variety of configurations. The shape and contours of the seating elements facilitate a wide range of possible groupings. They can be placed together, either to accommodate privacy or to invite communication; they can be both individual and private, or social and open.

Seating Stones are equally versatile when it comes to multi-purpose usage, offering a diversity of options for placement: from offices, waiting rooms, lobbies and meeting spaces to use in the home. In all situations the configuration of the seating elements can be arranged to suit individual spaces and the desired 'connectivity' of the users.

Inspired by the bright and varied natural fabrics produced by the Incas of Latin America, Seating Stones can be upholstered in a wide variety of fabrics and colours. Furthermore, the fabric types and colours can be mixed, creating different appearances and textures in each element, or in a grouping of individual seats. The fabrics of the Seating Stones can therefore reference a simple, individual stone, or alternatively resemble a mixed formation of richly coloured minerals.

Photography by H. G. Esch

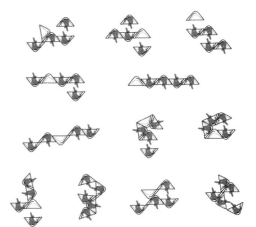

152

Serac Bench

Zaha Hadid Design

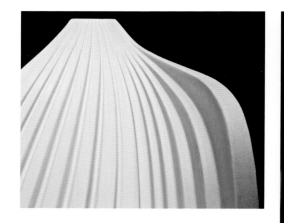

Client	LAB 23
Design	Zaha Hadid, Patrik Schumacher
Design Team	Filipa Gomes, Paolo Flores, Maha Kutay, Woody Yao
Dimensions	H45/70 (seat/back) x L250 x W80cm
Materials	Quartz resin
Colour	Grey/white

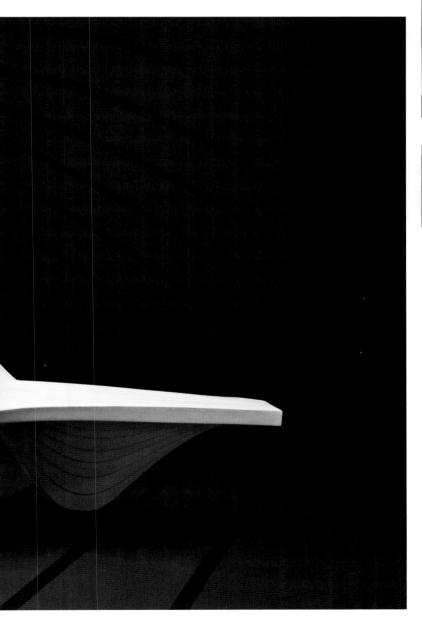

Developed as an urban sculpture for seating and resting, the Serac Bench seamlessly integrates with its context. Its striated articulations emerge from the landscape, each layer taking its own unique trajectory in reaction to latent forces that disperse – and ultimately coalesce – the many strata of the bench to generate its overall formal composition. The design rediscovers the fluid, continuous nature of Hadid's work – exploring relationships between solid and void, object and ground, form and function; an evolutionary lineage that is evident throughout her repertoire.

The bench has been developed in resin quartz, a tough and durable material that when shaped into a more curvaceous form, transitions into a softer, fluid and tactile surface. The sparkling crystal within the quartz balances stunning light-play with mesmerising depth.

Photography by Jacopo Spilimbergo

Series 7 Chair
Fritz Hansen

Designer	Arne Jacobsen
Dimensions	H44/78 (seat/back) x W50 x D52cm
Materials	Beech inner veneer, outer veneer in maple, walnut, Oregon pine, beech, elm, cherry, oak, black oak or ash, steel tube base, black synthetic material leg ferrules
Colour	Coloured ash (lazur), or lacquered in white, light grey, dark grey, black, yellow, orange, red, petrol blue or sage green

The Series 7 designed by Arne Jacobsen is by far the most popular chair in the history of Fritz Hansen in terms of sales, and perhaps also in furniture history. The pressure-moulded veneer chair is a further development of the classic Ant chair. The four-legged stackable chair can be seen as the culmination of the use of the lamination technique – refined to perfection during the 1920s and '30s by Søren C. Hansen, the grandson of the founder of the firm, Fritz Hansen. The visionary Arne Jacobsen exploited the possibilities of lamination to perfection resulting in the iconic shape of the chair.

Series 7 represents the chair with the widest range of applications in the Fritz Hansen collection. It is lightweight and stackable and offers options including armrests and castors. The architect offers stacking chairs in nine different types of wood, each with its own unique wood grain pattern, reflecting a comprehensive palette of natural wood tones and hues. What's more, they also offer the same chairs in a range of painted versions, in truly distinctive colours to complement the whole range of interior décor, whether at home or in the office.

Photography courtesy of the designer

Shell Games
Griffin Enright Architects

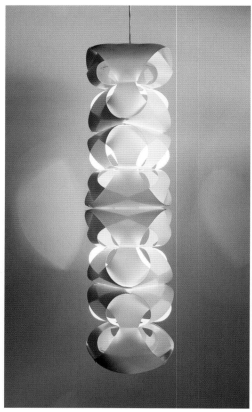

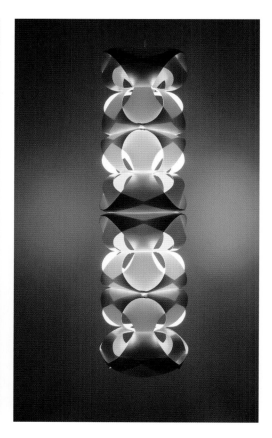

Dimensions	H122cm x diameter 30cm
Materials	.03mm high-impact white styrene

"Shell Games" is a new collection of lamps that explores the structural capacities of semi-translucent, thin-shell tectonics, while creating gradients of light. Through the repetition of a geometric module, a shell system of involution generates an exceedingly strong yet light shell. Despite the thinness of the material, the form of the modules allows the shape of each lamp to be self-supporting and rigid. The geometry also creates a play of solid and void, creating optical illusions as the viewer moves around the light. This duality allows the lamps to create patterns of light and shade on environments surrounding the lamps. The form is then dually functional as both a structural module and a three-dimensional light filter.

Dimensions   H30cm x diameter 76cm

Materials   .03mm high-impact white styrene

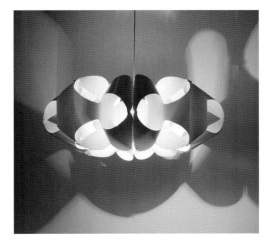 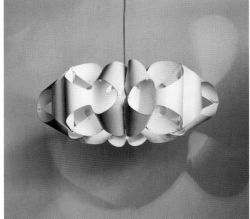 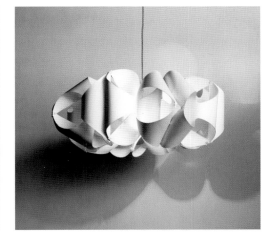

Lepido and Ranuncu are the two prototypes shown here; one is a chandelier and the other is a vertical hanging lamp. They are both made from .03 mm high-impact white styrene fastened together with nylon pop rivets. Incandescent lamps wash a warm light over and through the cool white styrene, creating light gradients from blue to orange. The shells are assembled to generate both directed task lighting, as well as ambient effects on surrounding surfaces.

Photography by MAK Center, Los Angeles and Nanao Shimizu

Shelving
Griffin Enright Architects

Dimensions	L350 x D35 x H48cm
Materials	5cm-thick birch timber

This floating shelf made from 5cm-thick birch timber is integrated into narrow steel pipe columns to create a divider that distinguishes living and dining areas. In the case of the model on this page, the shelf replaced a wall in the home, as the renovation was designed to open up the home, creating a loft-like feel. The shelving unit, integrated into the structure, works as an open divider. While it distinguishes the programmatic components of the home, it also unites the space, as a central, sculptural element. The long proportions of the shelf are unexpected, and focus attention towards the expansive view through the rear façade of the home.

Photography by Benny Chan Fotoworks

Shimmer Table and Chair
Gary Marinko

The Shimmer Table and Chair are paradigmatic of design-led research undertaken by the Advanced Timber Concepts Research Centre (ATC), a joint venture between the University of Western Australia and the Government of Western Australia's Forest Products Commission, whose overarching mission is to develop exemplary practices in the use of plantation and native timber in the context of environmental and industry sustainability.

Manufactured in native Western Australian eucalypt species of Karri, Jarrah and Sheoak, they exploit the strength and aesthetic character of these timbers to produce elegant, lightweight forms of great durability.

The Shimmer Table is designed to complement the Shimmer Chair, and makes its own point on light and minimal structure and form. Distinctive timbers and finishes are paired with sophisticated joinery techniques, resulting in a lean, functional form.

Dimensional constraints allow for the table's legs to be made from 25mm timber sections and the tabletop from a variety of high-tech materials and finishes. The tabletop is a strong contemporary counterpoint to the tradition of timber, while these new materials provide stiffness with light weight.

Dimensions	H72 x L175 x W87.5cm
Materials	Juvenile Karri timber legs; laminated, painted, carbon fibre or fibreglass top

The suitability of the constraints was tested through the making of physical and digital models of the table, which tested the aesthetic and constructional parameters of the project. When the design team was satisfied with the result of these exercises, a suite of technical drawings was produced to facilitate the production of the table prototype. The tabletop will be available in a variety of finishes.

Dimensions H83 x D50 x W42cm

Weight Less than 3kg

Materials Jarrah, Karri and Sheoak timber

Constructed from solid timber and utilising the inherent qualities of Western Australian hardwoods in combination with sophisticated joinery techniques, the Shimmer Chair pairs a refined aesthetic with extreme durability. It grew out of the observation that the local furniture manufacturers discarded timber that had a cross section of 20mm x 20mm or less. In an effort to carry out the design according to sustainable practice, the architect adopted this as the maximum component size.

Traditional timber furniture tends to be heavy, stiff, flat and rely on upholstery for comfort. This chair was to be light, flexible, textured and comfortable, while still being constructed from only solid timber. The timber species Jarrah and particularly Karri, which has long straight grain and great strength, were suitable candidates. Sophisticated jointing techniques were applied to the small timber sections to enable three-way joints to occur; the architect knows of no other timber chair constructed completely from such small square section components.

Other manufacturing techniques such as steam-bending and surface-milling were also used, and combined to fabricate the distinctive woven back. All components were sized to allow them to flex so that comfort was an integral characteristic of the components rather than applied through upholstery. The surface-milling applied to the seat battens provides the distinctive textured surface that 'shimmers'. In the final analysis, the chair relies on being an integrated structure where all the joints and members work together to provide strength and flexibility.

Photography by Leon Bird and Gary Marinko

SIRAP Shelves
Objects by Estudio Carme Pinós

The SIRAP series of shelves are manufactured from a single piece of 1.5mm-thick steel that has been folded into a corbel-like form. The S series has a depth of 12cm and can be used for the storage of small items, as well as a support for paintings. The M series is available in three different sizes and finishes, allowing a functional and versatile design ideal for storage of objects and books. At 30cm deep, multiple units of the L series can be mounted together to obtain a long, continuous shelf, making SIRAP L a versatile piece capable of supporting digital media systems and large books. SIRAP COLOR is available in different lengths and shades. Combining them permits a variety of aesthetic options with an attractive decorative appeal. In all series, the steel is cut by laser.

Dimensions	W60 x D12 x H8.2cm (SIRAP S)
	W60, 90 or 120 x D22 x H15cm (SIRAP M)
	W98 x D30 x H21cm (SIRAP L)
	W60, 90 or 120 x D22 x H15 cm (SIRAP COLOR)
Material	1.5mm steel plate
Weight (per unit)	2.1kg (SIRAP S)
	3.8kg (SIRAP M60)
	5.7kg (SIRAP M90)
	7.6kg (SIRAP M120)
	8.35kg (SIRAP L)
	3.8kg (SIRAP COLOR 60)
	5.7kg (SIRAP COLOR 90)
	7.6kg (SIRAP COLOR 120)
Colours	White powder coating (SIRAP S, M and L)
	Dark grey powder coating with metallic effect (SIRAP S, M and L)
	Yellow powder coating (SIRAP COLOR 60)
	Red powder coating (SIRAP COLOR 90)
	Blue powder coating (SIRAP COLOR 120)

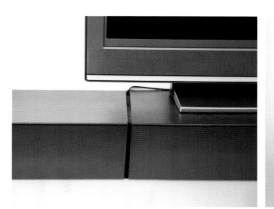

SitTable
UNStudio

Client	PROOFF
Design Team	Ben van Berkel, Caroline Bos, Juergen Heinzel, William de Boer, Machteld Kors, Martijn Prins, Daniela Hake
Dimensions	L550 x W175 x H75cm (Large)
	L400 x W175 x 75cm (Medium)
Materials	Large: White HPL tabletop with veneer white spraypainted sides, fabric seat, steel frame
	Medium: wood veneer dark oak tabletop, fabric seat, steel frame

Sit down, sit up, slouch, lounge, hang, repose, shift, twist, hunker, sit by yourself, sit together. UNStudio's SitTable is designed for the various ways in which people communicate. It refers to and extends the traditional role of the table as a social meeting place.

Through the cross-combination of usage possibilities, the SitTable offers a diversity of options for placement; it can be used in libraries, in airport lounges, waiting rooms, schools, as a display surface in exhibitions and shops and of course in the home. The SitTable offers a rich mix of qualities and a myriad of possibilities, not only in the context of placement, but also in the many tasks that can simultaneously be carried out at the table – both solitary and social, or a combination of the two. At any given moment, one person can be working at one section of the table, while other members of the family are enjoying a meal close by.

UNStudio has long been interested in hybrid forms of all scales, from large-scale mixed-use urban projects through to programmatic and volumetric transitions in public buildings and private residences. A similar approach is often taken to products designed by the studio, where hybridisation offers increased performance potential to a wide variety of users. The SitTable is a new addition to this family of designs, and is produced by Arco Contemporary Furniture.

Phototgraphy by Roel van Tour and Pim Top

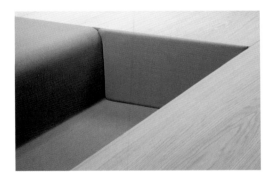

Soft Mosaic Collection

J. MAYER H. Architecture Design Research

A surprising new application for the celebrated Bisazza glass and ceramic tile company, this seating arrangement consists of glass mosaic on polyurethane foam. The architect has set the humble glass mosaic tile into sleek silhouettes in an illusory yet radically designed range of seating systems.

Photography by J.MAYER H.

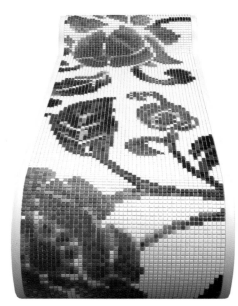

Design Team	Jürgen Mayer H., Heike Biechteler, Wilko Hoffmann
Dimensions	H88 x D111cm
Materials	Polyurethane foam, glass mosaic tiling

Spline Sideboard
Saaj Design

Design team   Andrew Bartholomeusz,
Sally Anderson, Claire Davy
with Damien Wright Studio

Dimensions   H45–72 x L680 x W47cm

Material   Coobah timber

The architect's brief for this piece was to explore the design of entertainment equipment with a fireplace and sideboard. Proportion, wit and movement for the sideboard in form and grain were key considerations. This catered to the pragmatic requirements of differing heights for dining and living spaces. As such, the piece connects the two spaces within an open plan.

Essentially, a 'found' Coobah tree has been deconstructed and reassembled. The sideboard 'log' appears to pierce the fireplace in an engaging and effective manner. The tree selected for this design was very specific and as such took some time to source. The construction technique involved thick veneering with blind mitred dovetails and a tung oil finish.

Photography by Andrew Bartholomeusz

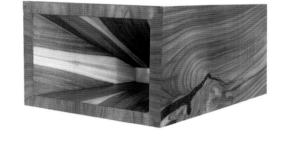

Studio series
UNStudio

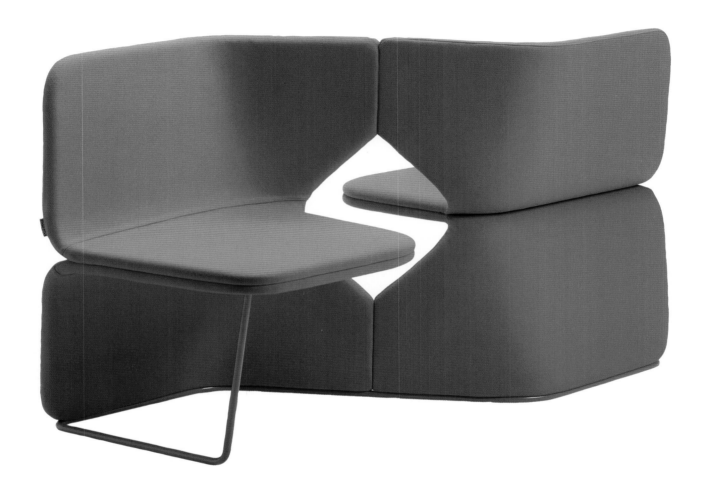

Client	OFFECCT
Design Team	UNStudio: Ben van Berkel, Caroline Bos, William de Boer, Mark Anthoni Friedhoff, Marcin Mejsak, Maurits Fennis
	Offecct: Anders Englund, Kurt Tingdal, Annette Mathiesen, Joachim Schubert, Mats Grennfalk
Materials	Upholstered moulded wood body, powder-coated steel frame, foam seat

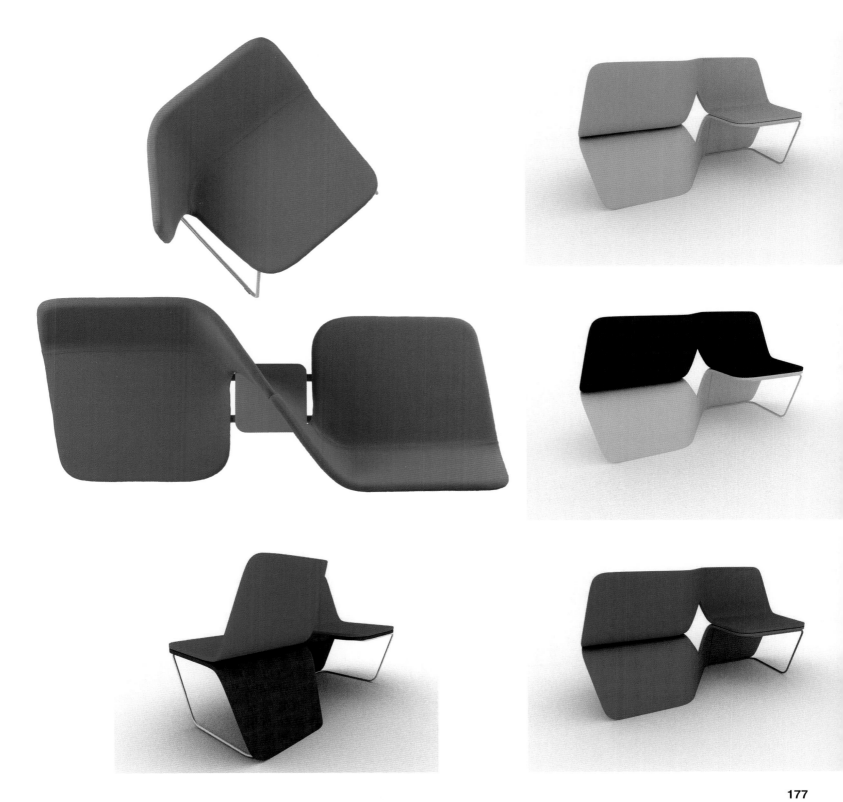

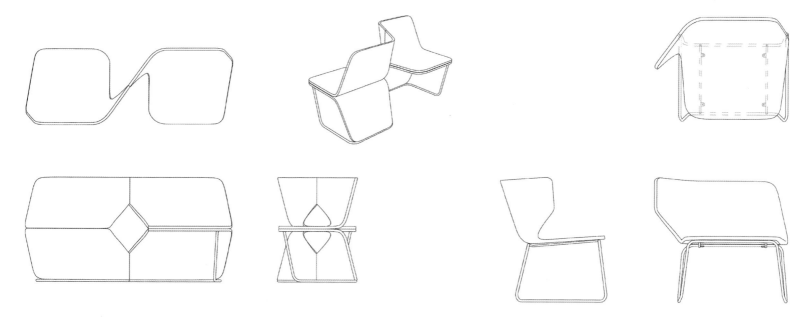

The *Studio* series for Offecct has been designed to allow for the creation of a number of seating units, each adapted to the needs of particular situations in terms of the number of seats as well as their arrangements and function in any given space. The designs allow for numerous group arrangements that can result in closed, semi-closed and open arrangements, allowing for versatility in communication and privacy.

The Studio *Twin* creates a seating element for communication and exchange, whereas the Studio *Easy chair Right* and *Easy chair Left* offer possibilities for the user to choose between open and private arrangements. The Studio Twin Beam creates opportunities for use in public spaces and for more playful organisations in public settings.

The *Studio* collection set-up has the potential for use in many varied settings, including airport waiting areas, lobbies, offices and libraries.

In order to create a sustainable product, the shell has been designed in such a way that the complete *Studio* collection can be produced with two mirrored shells. In addition, the shape of the shells and the frame allow these parts to be stacked for space-saving during transport. In accordance with Offecct's high demands on sustainability, effort has been put into choice of materials, energy, transportation and logistics to assure a product that has a minimal effect on nature.

Photography by Thomas Harrysson

Swatt Chaise Lounge

Swatt | Miers Architects

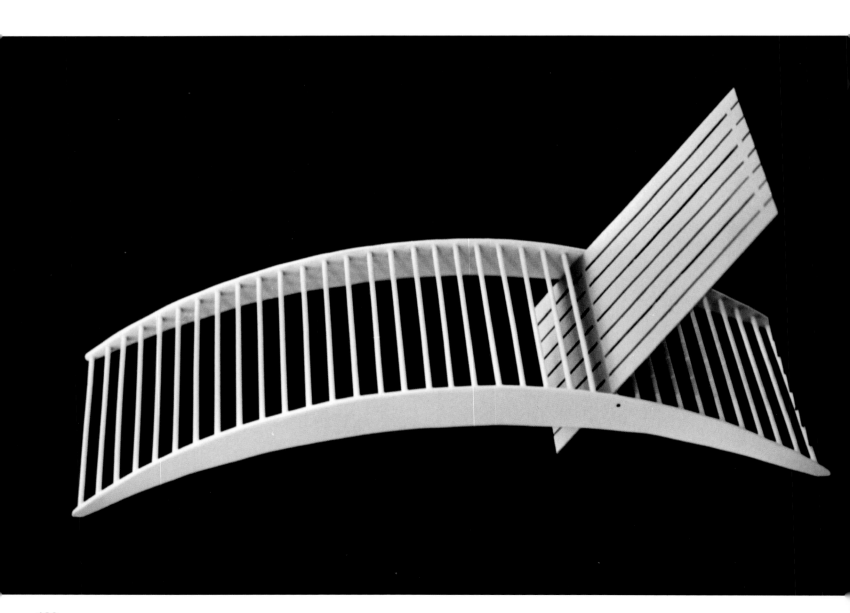

Designer	Robert Swatt
Dimensions	H31 x L178 x W61cm
Materials	Wood, steel
Colours	White, red

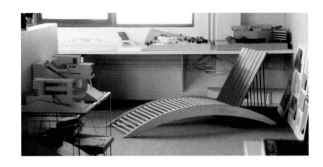

This chaise lounge was designed by Robert Swatt for the Outdoor Chair Show in Sausalito, California in 1987. It represents a natural extension of architectural design, expressing the ideas of arch, beam, compression, rhythm and contrast at the scale of the human body. It is at once both a functional piece of furniture and an elegant outdoor sculpture. The lounge prototype was hand-constructed by Swatt using wood dowels for the main body of the chair and wood planks for the back portion. Metal rods provide support for the vertical portion, and a single metal plate connects the chair back to the sides of the the wood frame.

Photography by Russell Abraham and Robert Swatt

Swiss Lakes Coffee Table Series
Philip Michael Wolfson with McCollin Bryan

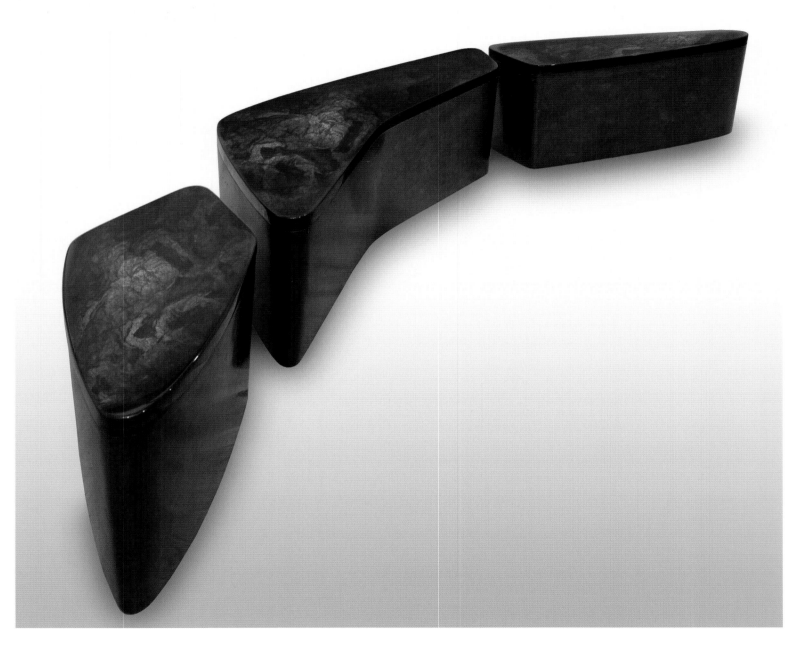

The examination of an unfamiliar topography engendered abstract notions, opening new depths of innovation and ideas about the impetus of revelation. The study began as an examination of the various maps available online, through the Swiss geological administration, offering a view not visible on a day-to-day basis. Relevant to each piece is the creation of a canvas of static versus dynamic forces, examining how the void and materiality rhythmically shape space; this is a modern representation of the tectonic folds of entire landscapes and the hidden depths of an unseen subterranean universe.

Photography by Maxim Nilov

Dimensions	H42cm x W30 x L85cm / W145
	L52cm / W91 x L54cm
Materials	Scagliola and cast resin exterior; gilded core

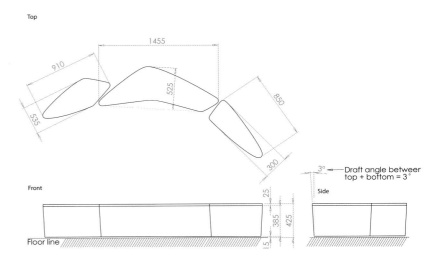

Ten Thousand Years Table
Saaj Design

This 12-seater dining table was inspired by the ribbon qualities of the house for which it was commissioned. The legs and tabletop flow as one continuous plane of timber. Careful attention to joint details, grain direction and proportion were all explored to reinforce this idea, employing origami techniques.

The qualities of the architectural space – light, bright and translucent – were used as a backdrop to the table, which is richly dark, solid, warm and organic. The petrified ancient red gum exudes a red-black colour that is hypnotic. This natural occurrence is very rare. The materiality of this table is, as the name would suggest, timeless. The construction technique involved thick veneering with blind mitred dovetails and a tung oil finish.

Photography by Damien Wright

Design team   Andrew Bartholomeusz,
               Sally Anderson with
               Damien Wright Studio
Dimensions   H75 x L330 x W120cm
Material   Ancient Red Gum timber from
               10,000-year-old fallen log

The Arachnid
Sander Architects

Designer   Whitney Sander
Dimensions   H74 x L203 x W91cm
Materials   Tube steel, plate steel, glass top

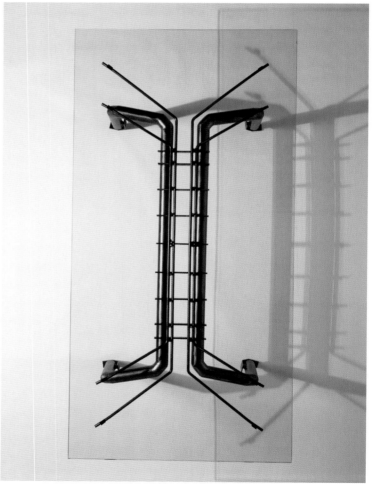

Designed by international award-winning architect Whitney Sander, this table has been dubbed 'The Arachnid' for its spider-like legs. Although the table was welded by a fabricator, the architect himself did the cutting, shaping and finishing of the steel, an accomplishment of which he is rightly proud. Very few architects have the opportunity to be hands-on in the construction of their designs, so creating this piece of furniture was particularly satisfying.

The table is made from welded raw steel with a glass top. The architect was exploring the idea of skeleton, bones and tendons, sinew and musculature. The influence of the spine, with its linked vertebrae, is particularly noticeable along the central length of the steel. The drawings for the table were created using the same techniques Sander still uses for designing a building: pencil and paper. Still, it is clear from the construction of the design that this project was approached from an architectural perspective, rather than a fabrication or furniture-making perspective.

Photography by Sharon Risedorph

TIND End Table
FINNE Architects

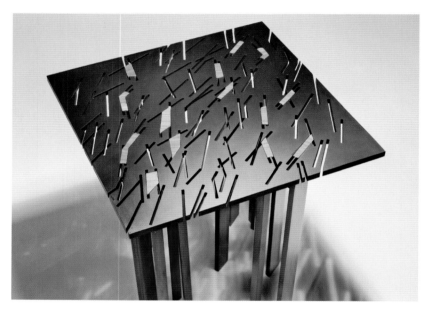

The TIND End Table is a small, eco-friendly table with a strong visual presence. The recycled steel top has been cut by water jet into an intricate pattern that creates vivid patterns of light and shadow. The shapes of the bamboo legs are determined by the patterning in the steel top – each of the fourteen legs passes through the steel top and is then cut flush. Seen from above, the carbonised bamboo creates an arresting pattern that is juxtaposed against the other perforations in the steel. "Every table should have fourteen legs!", claims the architect! Bamboo has become known as the quintessential 'rapidly renewable' raw material, since bamboo is a rapidly growing grass, not a wood product. The carbonised finish is created by heating the bamboo, which turns the light colour into a rich caramel.

Photography by Benjamin Benschneider

Design	Nils Finne
Manufacturer	Metalwork: Five Star Industries
	Woodwork: Seaboard Cabinet Company
Dimensions	H43cm; tabletop L38 x W38cm
Materials	Recycled steel, bamboo

titanium

Satoshi Okada architects

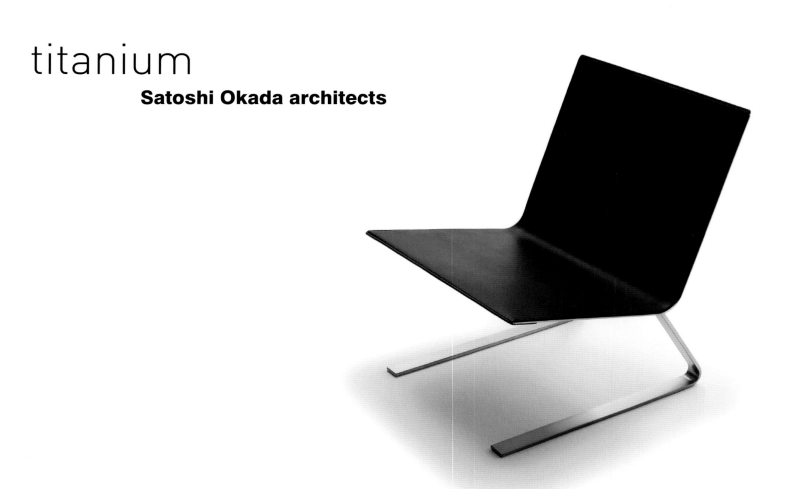

titanium was designed on a commercial basis for 'arti', a Tokyo-based furniture company. It is a lounge chair for private abodes, as well as public facilities. The design concept was to realise the most beautiful and comfortable chair with a simple composition by utilising the most advanced material and technology.

Today, the typology of chair design may seem to have reached saturation point. In such a difficult situation in terms of creating new design, the architect thought how he could realise the ultimate bending chair in the spirit of the Bauhaus tradition. The architect sought to utilise all the composite wisdom of the past into yielding the maximum effects by the minimum elements, which is indeed a reflection of modernity.

It is the first example internationally of a chair entirely comprising titanium. Chairs made from titanium have never appeared before, mainly because it is an extremely hard metal for handling, and because it is too expensive to use for mass production. In fact, it requires high-tech craftsmanship; and in Japan, there is only one company that can deal with it.

The chair is composed from two elements: one is a single plate, 3mm thick, bent for seat and back; the other is two legs of a flat bar, 45mm wide by 10mm thick, supporting the super-thin plate. The black leather, 5mm thick, is sewn to the metal to enhance human comfort. Because titanium is super-strong but elastic, the chair can be made of thin and small members to reduce the total weight to just 15kg.

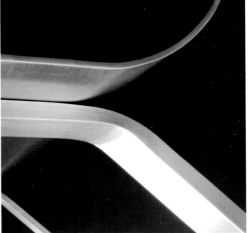

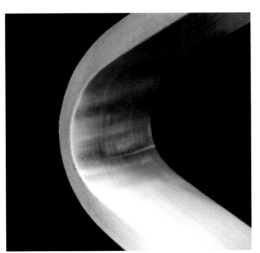

The movement in sitting is unique. The plate accepts the body sitting down with a moderate resilience. When legs are raised above the ground, the sitter can enjoy the comfortable swinging, as if sitting in the air. The plane for the back is always fitted to body movements with a temperate reaction. Even though it is only 3mm thick, it is enough to support a human body comfortably in a range of positions. It can withstand up to 200kg.

Photography by Satoshi Okada architects and arti

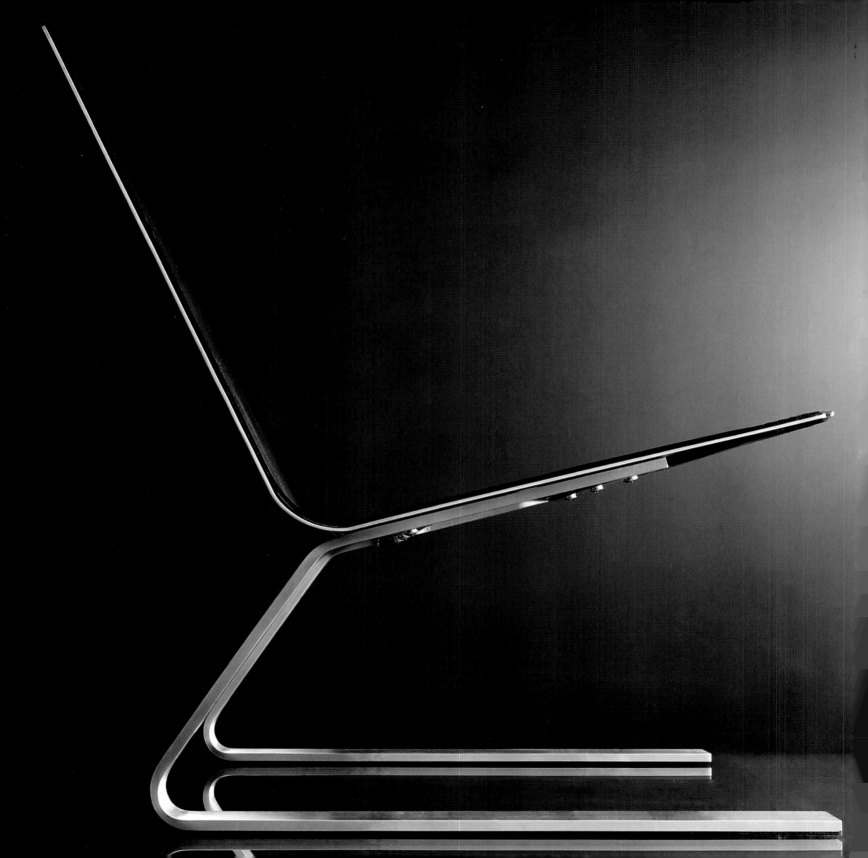

LOUNGE CHAIR SHOULD BE FLEXIBLE FOR SITTING POSITIONS OF HUMAN
BODY. THE METAL OF TITANIUM CAN FOLLOW THE MOVEMENTS ELASTICALLY.

titanium
S. OKADA

Designer   Satoshi Okada
Dimensions   H36/70 (seat/back) x W63 x D65cm
Materials   Titainuim plate, leather

Vortexx Chandelier
Zaha Hadid Design

The design language explored in the vortex is in line with a series of furniture pieces realised in collaboration with Sawaya & Moroni. Fluidity and seamlessness are conceptual terms that best describe the appearance of this 180cm-wide and 80cm-high chandelier. Its complex curvilinearity follows a double helix connecting its beginning to its end and therefore forming an endless ribbon of light. In plan, the object resembles a star with its protrusions pointing outwards from the centre, emphasising an imaginary centrifugal force.

Two transparent acrylic light spirals are inscribed in the chandelier's otherwise opaque surface. A recessed LED light strip provides animated and programmable light sensations. Direct as well as indirect light can be emitted to the environment optionally. Consequently, different lighting atmospheres may be created by the user in order to match the specific space in which the chandelier is installed. This new interior design language is fuelled by advanced digital design possibilities and manufacturing methods, such as CNC-milling and 3D printing. The user is invited to creatively explore its interactive qualities and respond to its unfamiliar aesthetics.

Photography by Zumtobel Lighting, rendering by Zaha Hadid Architects

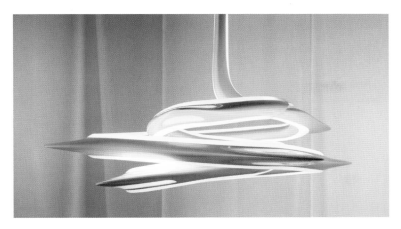

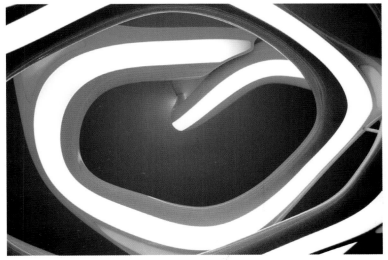

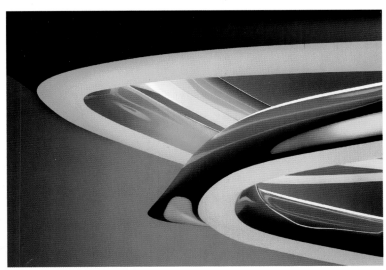

Design	Zaha Hadid, Patrik Schumacher
Designer	Thomas Vietzke
Dimensions	180cm diameter
Materials	Fibreglass, car paint, acrylic, LED

Walnut Dining Table
Stelle Lomont Rouhani Architects

The client wanted a custom table that would lend itself to intimate gatherings and larger dinner parties. The architect sourced a spectacular piece of American Claro Walnut, more than 100 years old, that would work in both a square and a rectilinear format. The table was designed to celebrate the large width of the wood slab. The architect sliced the slab in two so it could be positioned in a long format, to accommodate more guests. The live edge was preserved with traditional hand-planing and the natural shape was maintained. A clear flat finish was applied to the surface and the architect modeled the table with three-dimensional renderings to ensure that the geometry worked and that the base supports were in the right place.

The base is made from laminated ApplePly and black steel. The ApplePly references custom millwork in the house. The black steel base clings to a square opening cut into the ApplePly support fin, bending to support the weight of the table. The legs are set inboard of the top, to allow for comfortable seating in both configurations.

Photography by Frank Oudeman and renderings by Greg Tietjen

Design team	Frederick Stelle, Greg Tietjen, Eleanor Donnelly
Dimensions	H76 x L183 x W172cm
Materials	Walnut wood, laminated apple plywood, black steel

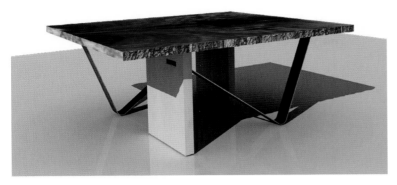

workplaysleep.01
Johnson Chou

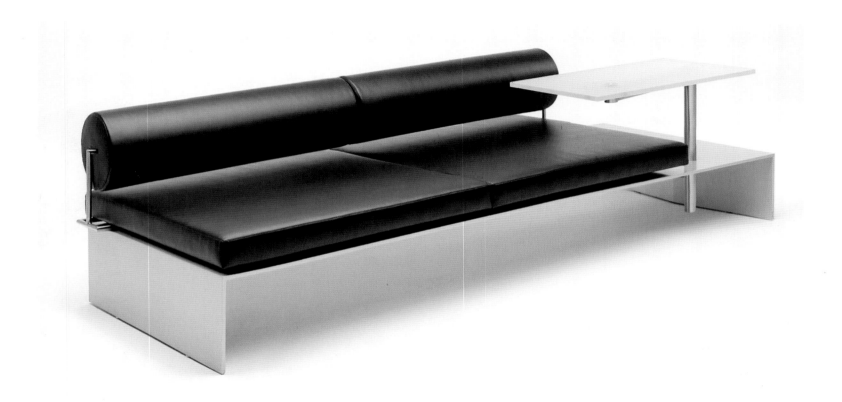

workplaysleep.01 reinterprets the principles of displacement and multi-functionality within the lexicon of sustainable design. It is an experiment in furniture design, responding to issues of material consumption. The project explores the possibilities of hybrid furniture within the context of rising land values and compact living spaces. It effortlessly assimilates three functions into a single multi-use object and thus eliminates the need for three separate pieces of furniture and three processes of production.

Using an innovative form of lightweight aluminium (manufactured by Alusion), the piece is constructed from a composite panel of recycled foam aluminum core and laminated with sheet aluminium. Despite its high embodied-energy content, this material has excellent morphing capabilities and can be recycled after use.

Designed to accommodate a twin-sized mattress, workplaysleep.01 allows for a variety of conventional and unconventional options for cushion material, including futon, air and spring mattress, foam and felt. Bubble wrap was selected for this prototype for its reusable capabilities; it is a ubiquitous, low cost/low impact material that can be easily renewed or replaced.

Acrylic, another recyclable material, is specified for the mattress platform and work surface to contrast with the texture and material qualities of aluminium. Utilising a combination of high and low-tech materials, workplaysleep.01 is designed to be adaptable and transformable for multiple functions and material options and can be easily disassembled into its component parts for transport or recycling.

Photography courtesy of the designer

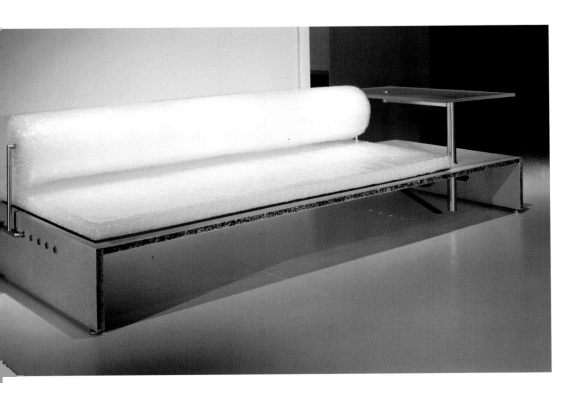

Dimensions   H71 x W191 x D99cm

Materials   Painted wood veneer, stainless steel, leather/ bubble wrap, acrylic

Z-Chair
Zaha Hadid Design

The design of the Z-Chair summarises the essence of contemporary design and the research developed by Zaha Hadid Architects over the last three decades. A simple three-dimensional gesture zigzags in space as part of the continued discourse between form and function, elegance and utility, differentiation and continuity.

Geometric abstractions inform the design's linear loop, which is articulated along its path in a language that alternates thin wire streams and large surfaces to provide both ergonomic affordances and inherent stability to the overall shape.

The dichotomy between the elegance of the composition and its articulation is negotiated through a subtle play of contrasting angular corners and wide, smooth curves. The resulting form echoes the calligraphic gestures of Hadid's two-dimensional works – a controlled brush stroke on a canvas, the perfect synthesis of an idea: the sketch.

Photography by Enrico Suà Ummarino

Client	Sawaya & Moroni
Design	Zaha Hadid, Patrik Schumacher
Design team	Fulvio Wirz, Mariagrazia Lanza, Maha Kutay, Woody Yao
Dimensions	H88 x L92 x D61cm
Material	Stainless steel

Zephyr Sofa

Zaha Hadid Design (manufactured by Cassina Contract)

Design	Zaha Hadid
	Patrik Schumacher
Design Team	Fulvio Wirz
	Mariagrazia Lanza
	Maha Kutay
Dimensions	L265 x W284 x H73cm
Materials	Lacquered fibreglass solid body, fabric upholstery

The sinuous shape of the Zephyr sofa is inspired by natural rock formations shaped by erosion: the application of subtractive processes that carve solid matter. The resulting formal language gives the Zephyr sofa increased ergonomic properties without compromising the design's fluidity or proportions, translating into a concept that allows for multiple seating layouts. The carved profile incorporates deep backrests and generous undercuts for unrivalled comfort. A lacquered finish applied to Zephyr's structural elements highlights every subtle nuance of its composition, and is contrasted by the tactile qualities of its bespoke upholstery and cushioning. Zephyr showcases Cassina Contract's unrivalled technical experience and longstanding tradition of artisan excellence.

Photography by Jacopo Spilimbergo

Index of architects and designers